Reimagining Spirit

Reimagining Spirit

WIND, BREATH, AND VIBRATION

Grace Ji-Sun Kim

CASCADE *Books* • Eugene, Oregon

REIMAGINING SPIRIT
Wind, Breath, and Vibration

Copyright © 2019 Grace Ji-Sun Kim. All rights reserved. Except for brief quotations in critical publications or reviews, no part of this book may be reproduced in any manner without prior written permission from the publisher. Write: Permissions, Wipf and Stock Publishers, 199 W. 8th Ave., Suite 3, Eugene, OR 97401.

Cascade Books
An Imprint of Wipf and Stock Publishers
199 W. 8th Ave., Suite 3
Eugene, OR 97401

www.wipfandstock.com

PAPERBACK ISBN: 978-1-5326-8924-6
HARDCOVER ISBN: 978-1-5326-8925-3
EBOOK ISBN: 978-1-5326-8926-0

Cataloguing-in-Publication data:

Names: Kim, Grace Ji-Sun, author.
Title: Reimagining Spirit : wind, breath, and vibration / Grace Ji-Sun Kim.
Description: Eugene, OR: Cascade Books, 2019 | Includes bibliographical references.
Identifiers: ISBN 978-1-5326-8924-6 (paperback) | ISBN 978-1-5326-8925-3 (hardcover) | ISBN 978-1-5326-8926-0 (ebook)
Subjects: LCSH: Holy Spirit. | Social justice. | Climate change.
Classification: BT121.2 K47 2019 (print) | BT121 (ebook)

Manufactured in the U.S.A.   NOVEMBER 7, 2019

Dedication to my youngest child,
Joshua Benjamin Ho-Jin Lee on his sixteenth birthday.
He has given me so much joy, and I want him to continue
to live with the joyful spirit in his heart.

Table of Contents

Acknowledgments ix

Introduction 1

Chapter 1: Global World, Spirit, and Han 9

Chapter 2: Spirit as Light 36

Chapter 3: Spirit as Wind and Breath 60

Chapter 4: Spirit as Vibration 78

Chapter 5: Spirit and Social Action 99

Conclusion 123

Bibliography 137

Acknowledgments

My life as scholar, minister, speaker, and mother revolves around the Spirit. The presence of the Spirit in my life has proved to be ever more apparent as time goes on, continually surprising me in its profound influence. These personal encounters with the Spirit have compelled me to share my experiences and write this book.

There have been many other people who have contributed to the evolution and completion of this book. First, I thank my editor, Rodney Clapp, and managing editor, Matthew Wimer, at Cascade Books, for their counsel in making this book a reality. Then, there are my colleagues at Earlham School of Religion, whom I am deeply thankful for, as their endless advocacy and positivity sustained my determination throughout the writing process. I am grateful to my friends, Dr. Joseph Cheah, Rev. Mark Koenig, Dr. Donald McKim, Dr. James Logan, Dr. Susan Shaw, Rev. Jesse Jackson, and Dr. Graham Joseph Hill, who have been immense sources of inspiration and strength.

I am grateful for graduate students Leigh Waltz, Caroline Morris, and Daniel Mudd for their assistance in editing important sections of this book, as well as my research assistant, Bruce Marold, whose astute editing helped shape this into a more persuasive read. In addition, I would like to thank my gracious niece, Naomi Faith Bu, who provided valuable insights from a contemporary perspective, emending the writing to be further inclusive and grounded.

I cannot forget my family, which has been a continual source of support while I was writing this book. My sister Karen, brother-in-law Bruce, and nephew Matthew have provided a place to rest and eat while writing portions of this book. And I am thankful for my husband, Perry, who stood by me as I first began and then finished this book (and never complained

Acknowledgments

about the mess on my desk), and my three lovely children, Theodore, Elisabeth, and Joshua, who encouraged me through their energizing spirit. I am so grateful for my colleagues, friends, and family, whose support during this journey will forever be remembered, as their presence has now become inextricably embedded into this work of writing.

Introduction

I AM CAPTIVATED BY mystery. I have always confronted the unsolved problem, the unrevealed truth, and that thrilling uncertainty with a kind of confidence that was at times unprecedented or credulous. Yet the subject that has loomed over my unwavering nerve is also that of the greatest significance; it is the most enigmatic piece of the puzzle within my own spirituality: the Holy Spirit.

Like many others, I experience the Holy Spirit as a mystery. While it has been referenced routinely in historical texts and modern discourse, this entity is seldom understood. I have come a long way in my relationship to an understanding of the Holy Spirit, moving from a place of blind acknowledgment to a place of informed passion.

In my religious practice, I return time and time again to a position of investigation when studying the Spirit. In doing so, I try to make sense of the problems we face in the present day while also elucidating troubles in the past. It is a daunting task. However, this experience evokes challenging, powerful, and deeply personal insights that induce rare chances to recall lost memories and embrace new risks. Here, I am able to confront my whole past while continuing to embrace the future.

This book offers a distinct approach to the Holy Spirit. As you explore new territories, reach new communities, and travel the vastness of our Earth, you will recognize that the Spirit's presence transcends time, place, culture, and religion. It is completely free; it is important to be open to this notion as we explore together and create a pneumatology that speaks inclusively, on a local, global, and universal level.

Reimagining Spirit

Spirit's World

The world is filled with the Spirit. One can feel the presence of the Spirit everywhere. As the rate of globalization expands and travel becomes increasingly accessible, we will become witnesses to how the Spirit works in different communities other than our own. We can begin to see and experience the work of the Spirit in our churches, our communities, and our families as the world continues to largen and diversify. The Spirit lives in this ever-adapting world through its constant, unbroken presence in our lives.

As we see the work of the Spirit around the globe, some questions arise: Does the Spirit belong to Christianity or does it belong to the world? Does such a question offer a better understanding of the Holy Spirit within and around us? Would this, in turn, inform our global comprehension of the Holy Spirit as a Christian vision of a universal human perception? The Spirit is God, and no one community can hold it or possess it. It is an unbound entity that is free to move as it wishes in the world. The gift of life and the struggle for equality in the ecosystem of life is sustained by the Spirit's power, and this cannot simply be contained in the church or within Christianity.

The Spirit manifests itself in the world. The Spirit comes to the whole world as it manifests itself in nature.[1] Most Christians tend to see it in relation to the Trinity, while other faiths might see it in relation to the cosmos or the body. Our lives are enhanced when we are aware of this presence and when we make room for its participation, allowing it to permeate our lives, moving and working within us.

Whenever we welcome and embrace the Spirit within our lives, we draw closer to God. God is in all things because all things are in God. God is ubiquitous: God is wherever creation is.[2] God is all around us. The Spirit empowers us and possesses us to act, taking care of each other and creation. It begs us to deepen our knowledge of God and challenges us to search the world for more ways of speaking about the divine.

The Spirit is not owned by anyone, and we certainly cannot say that it is in the sole possession of Christians. People of different faiths also experience and articulate the Spirit in their lives. We know this because people have shared their stories and practices that involve the Spirit. The Spirit

---

1. Hodgson, *Christian Faith*, 140.
2. McFague, "Dearest Freshness Deep Down Things," 117.

Introduction

cannot be contained as the Spirit is free and moves where it will. Christianity cannot put a lock on how God is experienced by us or revealed to others. God says, "I Am Who I Am" (Exod 3:14), which shows the movement of God, unconstrained by human dictates or doings.

Christianity has tried to monopolize the divine Spirit for far too long through European colonization and cultural assimilation. The church has tried to teach the false sentiment that it is only Christianity that has the Spirit and that all other "spirits" or experiences of the "spirit'" are untrue. As Christianity colonized different parts of the world, it spread its own version of God and the Spirit to overcome Islam, Hinduism, and Buddhism. Christianity presented itself as the superior religion—the only "real" belief system—which understood and had a hold on the divine Spirit. The message was and is: "Only Christianity can provide understanding and comprehension of the Spirit." To experience and understand the Spirit (they said), one had to follow Christianity. In this modern world, where information and technology disseminates ever more rapidly throughout a diversifying world, is it not time to rethink, re-examine, and challenge these long-held beliefs and attitudes?

Whenever Christianity plays an imperialistic role, it tends to view itself as superior to belief systems where the culture's traditions are passed on orally rather than textually. As a result, the stranger becomes the other, an estranged being who is somehow deemed less worthy. However, those who maintain this perception fail to see the beauty that can only be discovered once they begin to recognize the stranger within themselves.

We understand that this Spirit cannot be constrained and withheld by Christianity. We cannot imprison the Spirit within Christianity and present it to the world as if only Christians can encounter the Spirit. Christians are not the center by any overwhelming margin, and we cannot hold onto something that "hovers over the surface of the water" (Gen 1:2) and that declares, "I will be what I will be" (Exod 3:14). The Spirit is boundless, and it is both naïve and ignorant for Christians to claim that it is only their Spirit that is holy. In so many ways, the Spirit opens rather than closes the door for us to be in conversation with the world's religions. Thus, the presence of the Spirit creates an "open space" wherein we encounter *the other*—in fact all others—in full dignity and uniqueness.

The Christian doctrine of the Spirit's freedom is vital as we hope to open dialogue among different faith traditions. As the Spirit moves in our lives and gives us breath, life, and sustenance, we become open to all the movements of the Spirit in all parts of the world, in all traditions, all cultures, and all religions. This is a movement of the Spirit that no one person, doctrine, or church can stop.

The "Holy" in Spirit

The Spirit is experienced and understood by people all over the globe, from various religions and cultures. However, in Christianity, we decided to add the word *holy* in front of the word *Spirit*, which then paved the road to make the Spirit exclusive to Christianity. The addition of *holy* before the word Spirit makes it clear that the Spirit is set apart from other things in the seen world. The *Holy* Spirit is no ordinary thing.

Within Christianity, God's Spirit is called *Pneuma Hagion*—Holy Spirit. The power of God is understood to be the Spirit of God moving in the world around us to change us and help us live in the pursuit of greater justice.

As we move into the New Testament, we will see that it is made explicit that the Spirit is now associated with Jesus, who lived and worked under the power of the Holy Spirit (Luke 4:1). Not only was his birth initiated by the Holy Spirit (Matt 1:18), but the Holy Spirit was seen to descend upon Jesus at his baptism (Mark 1:10).[3] After Jesus ascended to heaven, he sent the Spirit to the people. The Spirit of God that was active in Jesus' life is the same Spirit that is active in ours.

Spirit Walks with You

There was a mystery about the Spirit during the time of Jesus, and that mystery still remains. No one fully comprehends the Spirit. We may never fully comprehend the Spirit or the Spirit's action in our lives. But this may not be a bad thing, because if we could fully comprehend it and come to know everything about it, then it would not be God.

As in the past, the modern church continues to believe that the Spirit belongs to them. They teach that the Spirit, along with its gifts and its grace, can only be accessed in the church. Today, some of us are recognizing that the walls of the church cannot bind the Spirit and that this ideology is actually detrimental to those it involves and targets. The Spirit, God's

---

3. Pungur, *Theology Interpreted*, 84.

INTRODUCTION

eschatological presence and power, guides the church, but it is the *ruach*[4] who is ever-present in creating and in redeeming, present in the words of Jesus and those who follow him.

The understanding of the Spirit was not always clear to the people around Jesus and those following him. Even the disciples were not in full knowledge of what the Spirit meant. Toward the end of his ministry, Jesus promised his disciples that the Holy Spirit would be their constant companion (John 14:26) after he inevitably had to leave them. They were told that the Spirit would comfort them, help them, and guide them (Luke 12:12). After the crucifixion and the resurrection, Jesus the Christ gave the Spirit to the disciples by breathing on them (John 20:22).

The early Christian communities consistently spoke of the Spirit as the motherly, regenerative breath and power of God within creation. They believed that the Hebrew feminine name of the Spirit, *ruach*, was a linguistic clue to certain feminine-specific characteristics of God as Spirit. As these early Christians rightly understood, God transcends gender. Their point was not that God was a female deity but that it is appropriate to refer to God's mystery, love, and power in both masculine and feminine terms.[5]

The Spirit is God's presence as well as the eschatological presence. It guides the eschatological community of those born again through faith in Christ. The Spirit speaks to the church in times of crisis (Rev 2–3), enabling them to preach the word of God (Luke 12:12). It also builds up the church by empowering members to maintain their unity (Acts 4) and serve the common good with their gifts of ministry (1 Cor 12).[6]

The Spirit liberates, transforms, reconciles, empowers, and assures. The Spirit is powerful and uses its capacity to empower us to do God's work. The church is reminded that to be "in Christ" is the same as being "in the Spirit" (1 Cor 12:3).

Hybrid Pneumatology

Contextual theology sees religious pluralism as an exception rather than the norm. Liberation is not imposing a new idea; it is a response to voices within and outside of the biblical tradition.[7] A hybrid pneumatology is not

---

4. *Ruach* is the Hebrew word used for Spirit in the Old Testament.
5. Wallace, "Spirit," 241.
6. Min, *Solidarity of Others*, 116.
7. Sugirtharajah, *Bible and the Third World*, 262.

bound within the limits of Christianity when it searches for contextual methods of understanding the Spirit. Hybrid pneumatology is Christianity remaining bound to the Spirit itself rather than to the Spirit of a philosophical ideology. It can open other religious sources to illuminate our understanding of the Spirit. As we talk about God and Spirit, it is crucial to contemporary theological discourse that we are not just open to other religious views and understandings but also respect these beliefs within the landscape of our own.

Many people live in the in-between space of different groups: different generations, different social networks, and different cultures. This is of course not a set space but rather an unbounded, porous setting that allows its residents to move freely. In respect to religious differences, we must understand that despite different belief systems, there can never be a wholly monolithic framework. These things exist dynamically in reaction and relation to the conditions they are set in. It is in this in-between space that we find divine existence. The reign of God is built in the areas between us; therefore, that space becomes sacred ground. The Divine exists in a space beyond our imagination. We can begin to theologize and encounter the Divine in this space,[8] which is open, vibrant, and infinite.

This re-envisioned pneumatology works toward eliminating destructive habits, such as racism and sexism, both of which are heavily ingrained within all dominant modern societies. In turn, the understanding of *Chi* vibration, breath, light, and Spirit will empower all people to live holistic lives while working towards making this world a better place for all those who inhabit it.

Book Outline

The Spirit is not part of the observable world, and because we cannot see it or touch it, we will never fully uncover its mysteries. However, we can uncover the ways that the Spirit is present in our world by examining our experiences with light, wind, and vibration. This book will examine these ways of experiencing the Spirit in the world, and in connecting the Spirit with creation, it will ultimately emphasize the great importance of creation care.

Environmental justice has not been a priority in many of our lives. This book invites us to participate in taking care of all of God's creation.

8. Kim, "What Forms Us," 95.

Introduction

The same Spirit who was present at creation reminds us of God's continued presence in creation today. Though we are collectively ignoring the cries of the Earth, the Spirit is begging us to take care of the Earth, for in doing so, we are taking care of each other and God. Climate change is *the* monumental issue of our time, and in order to work towards improving the state of our Earth, we need to take a closer look at our theology and pneumatology, because how we view God has a direct impact on how we take care of the planet.

This book will follow three movements: light, wind, and vibration. These three movements will work toward deepening the understanding of God as Spirit, which I hope will inspire all of us to become involved in creation care and sustainable practices. The book will begin with contextual pneumatology and will subsequently explore Spirit as light, wind, and vibration. The chapters will be a biblical/theological study of the work of the Spirit—the overall "work of the Spirit"—illustrated from Scripture, history, culture, and doctrine. These chapters will each be tied to social justice issues, such as climate change, racism, and sexism. Adopting the living expression of the Spirit's actions as light, wind, and vibration will inspire us to work for change and move towards greater equity and good.

This book challenges an assumption some Christians make that the Holy Spirit is only available to baptized Christians, promoting the view that the Spirit exists in all cultures and faiths. God's affirmation, "I WILL BE WHO I WILL BE," (Exod 3:14) illustrates that the Spirit cannot be restricted by one religious group and is present in all creation and among all people, including "the other."

We live in a global world, and therefore, it is crucial that we talk about the Spirit in ways that are and can be experienced globally. We live in a world where divergent cultures and religions feud over legitimacy; the need to coexist compassionately becomes essential as we seek environmental and social aid.

This book is biblically and theologically grounded, tackling one of the most important topics of our day. The environmental path that society has chosen is a clear path to destruction. Therefore, it is necessary that we take actions that are informed by faith and beliefs. It is crucial that corrective measures are initiated immediately. We have been taught that the Spirit is gentle, that it is the comforter that Jesus sends to us, but it is important to recognize that for all the Spirit's kindness, its power is unimaginable. The power of the Spirit will transform our lives, our ways of thinking, and our experiences of God. These transformative experiences will offer us the tools we need to live sustainably in nature as God's creation and God's love.

This book will provoke readers into higher consciousness and push them to think of experiencing and referring to the Holy Spirit in deeper and more innovative ways. It will awaken readers to the Spirit's presence in their lives, helping all to recognize the power it holds—reinvigorating and surprising us with newfound knowledge, opportunities, power, and passion.

CHAPTER 1

Global World, Spirit, and Han

Pentecost

SOMETHING HAPPENED TO THE Spirit between Pentecost and the time of the early church fathers. At Pentecost, the crowd saw a lively and fiery Spirit whose power was so formidable that it could burn down a house in the blink of an eye. The Spirit came down upon legions of people, giving them life as tongues of fire burned on their heads. It was a wondrous and surprising day! For those not present in the upper room, the flaming tongues of the Spirit were things of fantasy and make-believe—but on Pentecost, it became a reality before their eyes. The powerful and living Spirit of God came down on the people, giving them a new life, a new beginning, and a new future.

Yet, this Spirit faded away and seemingly vanished from the church over the next few centuries. How could this have happened to the powerful life-giving Spirit, which was promised to move, shake, and alter the world? How did the church lose its excitement and belief in the Holy Spirit? How did the discourse surrounding the Holy Spirit become so obscure and insignificant that the church subsequently neglected to discuss it for hundreds of years?

The Spirit became the step-sister of theology, pushed to the margins as Christology took center stage and the Gospels and letters of Paul were written and shared. Theologians discarded the Spirit soon after, apparently disinterested in any related conversation, resulting in a loss to Western theology.

Perhaps this issue can be attributed to rational thinking, dualism, patriarchy, and Eurocentrism. In a world where feasibility is valued over wisdom and emotional intellect, it is easy to disregard the Spirit, for the Spirit moves people and transforms the world in a way that cannot be explained simply or rationally. The existence of patriarchy necessitates logical order and hierarchy, and in such a culture, it is easy to ignore the movement and presence of the Holy Spirit. Western thought generally focuses on rational behavior and repudiates mysterious, irrational, feminine, non-Eurocentric, and non-Christian ways of being and interpreting God. With this in mind, it is no surprise that the Western church has long disregarded the Spirit.

But now, as the church is given a younger, progressive breath, it is slowly moving away from male, Eurocentric ways of thinking, and is shifting towards a place where the global Christian identity is inclusive and diverse. This is imperative, as the health of Christianity at large depends on the contribution of all voices from around the world. We must reclaim the life-giving Spirit that vibrates and breathes new life into us and the whole world; the Spirit, which is the light, has the power to illuminate a world eclipsed by *han* and collective suffering.[1]

In this book, I am seeking to discover a global understanding of the Spirit by pursuing and excavating truths from my own heritage as a Korean-American theologian. Through exploring the rich, spiritual Asian tradition of *chi*, which offers an inquisitive and insightful look at the Spirit, along with the biblical tradition's vision of the Spirit as light, wind, and vibration, I intend to share my truth and the truth of the Spirit.

Global World

It is very difficult for a religion to be culturally neutral. As the Hebrews wandered in the desert, waiting for God to direct them toward the promised land, they recognized that their practices and understanding of YHWH were influenced by their neighbors. We live in relation to one another. There is not one person who is unaffected or uninfluenced by the cultures, practices, philosophies, and religious traditions of their neighbors. To understand the influence of our current culture, we need to examine the historical circumstances, traditions, and cultures that formed the doctrines of our Latin-based Eurocentric theology.

---

1. *Han* is a Korean term for unjust suffering. More analysis and explanation of this term will be given in chapter 5.

Global World, Spirit, and Han

The globalization of theology began with the Latin clergy, who made up the First Estate of the government of Christendom for much of its church history. Late Ancient and Medieval monarchs sent missionaries to northern Europe to convert the barbarian races. In the Age of Exploration, Jesuit missionaries were sent with the Conquistadors to the New World. Both Catholics and Protestants continue to send missionaries to frontiers in the Americas, Australia, and Oceana (Pacific Islands.)

Christian denominations proselytize the aboriginal world as if theirs were the only spiritual perspective and the only valid worldview. This imparted enduring consequences that have left the aboriginal peoples disenfranchised, ignored, and broken. The Christian world bulldozed into the aboriginal world with no regard, demonizing practices that existed for thousands of years. Christianity believed that its own doctrines were the true teachings of God and that everything else was simply false. Through intolerance and colonization, Christianity dominated the world, devaluing everything outside of their own culture, religion, and heritage, rendering it all illegitimate. Consequently, Christian doctrine and globalization are symbiotically interconnected, and the understanding of one requires the understanding of the other.

The globalization of European culture has exported a European way of understanding God and the Trinity. It is so powerful that many people around the world believe that God is a white male God. This image of God as a European has been brought to and often forced upon the late Christianized world. Anything divergent from this visage is thought by Christians to be blasphemous and an aberration of God. This way of thinking has ignored the traditions, spirituality, and cultures of peoples around the globe. It has preached to populations that their own spirituality and forms of being religious are "wrong." It has maligned any divergent, non-Western belief systems as primitive, animistic, and savage. We need to acknowledge this theological colonization and try to correct the many wrongs that have been done. The negative consequences of discrediting and destroying native lives and cultures have been overlooked and minimized for too long.

But now, for the first time in history, Christianity's presence is diminishing in Europe and the North.[2] As Christianity moves to the Global South, it is becoming ever more important to both represent and listen to non-white voices and have their perspectives included into Christianity. It

---

2. For more discussion on Christianity moving to the Global South, see Jenkins, *New Faces of Christianity*.

is now time to seek out and embrace a global understanding of a *theology of theologies* (roughly comparable to a *philosophy of theology*).

The vast majority of the world thinks about God without the resurrected Christ and with an immanent rather than transcendent Holy Spirit. It is time that we acknowledge this reality and begin to engage in conversation with worldwide partners to attain an informed ecumenical understanding of the Spirit. We need to push and expand the restrictive spiritual boundaries we have drawn to allow the Spirit to breathe, move, and blow as it wishes.

Some may think that this move will jeopardize Christianity. Others may think that it will alter Christianity. They may believe this revolution will bring bad spirits in and confuse our spiritual conviction. All this fear grows from the human inclination to fear the unknown, and this unhealthy frame of mind will ultimately lead to the weakening of one's faith. Fear enslaves us rather than enabling us to act freely. The Spirit is a gift to all people, purposed with the intention to inspire and enlighten us.

In the Old Testament, Joel reminds us that the Spirit was not only given to a small group of people but was poured onto all peoples. The Spirit moves as it wishes, and it cannot be captured or contained. Not even Christians can limit its activity, for the Spirit as light, wind, and vibration exists in all places and not just within Christian communities or churches. Just as the wind moves and blows in all directions, so does the Spirit.

Christianity has never been "purebred." It existed as an amalgam of varied cultural and religious understandings until the Reformation's search for doctrinal purity replaced syncretism. The Israelites who roamed around the desert recognized some borrowings when they "(de)spoiled the Egyptians."[3] Even the understanding of Hebrew wisdom seems to have been borrowed from the Egyptian concept of Isis, as there are too many similarities to ignore.[4]

My theology classes are made up of a diverse group of students, each with a unique set of values and beliefs. I have students who are Pentecostals, Presbyterians, Lutherans, and Unitarians. Most of my students are accustomed to this diversity; however, I can remember an instance where a student professed, to the dismay of other students in the class, that they

---

3. "Spoiling the Egyptians" is an expression used frequently in Augustine's writings, which alludes to learning and appropriating Egyptian technology and culture. Augustine is not the only Christian writer who used the term.

4. For more discussion on the similarities between Isis and Hokmah, see Kim, *Grace of Sophia*.

followed a "purer" Christianity. When I heard that, I was reminded of all the ways that pagan practices have influenced Christianity, which begs the question of whether there can even be this notion of a wholly "pure" Christianity. If we examine the traditions of Christmas and Easter, we can see that they have significant pagan influences. It is ironic that early missionaries adopted pagan customs into the "unofficial" canon of seasonal celebrations, but nonetheless, these footprints of other influences serve as an important reminder for all of us.

Theology has been used as a glue to hold empires together. This is especially true of the Catholic South America; the Anglican Africa outside of Egypt and the Mediterranean coast; and the Dutch (Boer) South Africa. As European[5] nations colonized and dominated different regions of the world, they brought their theologies to the peoples where no written tradition and little architectural tradition[6] existed, such as Canada and Australia.[7] Having the same religion or beliefs holds the colonized together and allows the conquerors to continue to maintain their power over the dominated people.

Constantine knew this well and put it into practice as he ruled his empire. Constantine was the Roman Emperor from 306 to 337 CE, and he was the first Roman emperor to convert to Christianity. He called the First Council of Nicaea in 325 CE as many Christians were fighting over doctrine regarding the nature of Jesus Christ. They congregated together to decide who he was; was he divine or was he just a human being? Christians thereafter used the Nicene Creed to profess their faith as well as to unite people and ensure that they would abide by one, singular faith. Having a common belief brought people together and lent a sense of cohesiveness. It was a touchstone for identifying heresies, and it brought the empire together as its inhabitants came to believe in the same God. In this way, Constantine made Christianity the religion of Europe, Northern Africa, and the

---

5. American empire-building had a special, theological flavor based on the notion of "exceptionalism," which in turn was based on the idea that the American continent was a New Jerusalem, the city on the hill, and conventional rules didn't apply. Europeans tended to be more pecuniary in their ambitions.

6. The content of aboriginal religion was embodied primarily by stories, plastic art, music, and dance.

7. We cannot accuse Christianity of being the only imperialistic religion. Islamic expansion and the Muslim religion were even more tightly bound together. The islands which became the Dutch East Indies were mission fields for Dutch Reformed Christianity as well as Hinduism, Buddhism, and ultimately, Islam.

Middle East—until the advent of Islam. This common religion, united with civil authority to create a monolithic Christendom, kept people together by having them believe in a common God.

This practice continued to be perpetuated throughout history by others like the Spanish and Portuguese conquistadors. As they colonized lands and added to their empires, they imposed their religion on those they conquered, requiring everyone to believe in the same God. Thus, white Catholic (Spain, Portugal, France, Belgium), Anglican (English), Dutch Reformed (Holland), and Evangelical (German Lutheran) theology[8] was forced upon the indigenous, conquered peoples around the world.

It is through differences in both Christian and non-Christian traditions that we begin to enrich our own way of understanding God. Contemplation, imagination, and re-envisioning are needed to move us toward an understanding of the kaleidoscopic cultures on this planet. These new social identities inform and transform theology with the times. Therefore, we must open ourselves up to indigenous forms of spirituality. It is essential to recognize the interconnectedness we have with the people, creatures, and environment of the world. Sallie McFague, a noted feminist eco-theologian, writes, "We are not separate, static individuals who choose to be in relations with other life-forms when we feel like it." We are part of the "intricate, changing cosmos that gave us birth and sustains us."[9] The recognition of our inevitable connectedness is a necessary step in understanding why it is we need to act with virtuosity. We are told to be kind, we are told to be generous, we are told to be truthful—but why? As we are all interrelated, we must act as brothers and sisters to all. Because if we ultimately aim to pursue unity on Earth, it can only be done through the ability to welcome strangers and accept them as an integral part of our lives.

This is in line with much of Asian thought and philosophy, which believes in the collective rather than the individualistic tendencies of the North American Protestant fundamentalists. Asians generally have prioritized community or communal understanding as the central aspect of how a society grows and maintains itself.

African Ubuntu theology believes that "I am because of who we are." It puts priority on others and being part of a community rather than on ourselves as individuals. Ubuntu theology teaches us about being self-aware

---

8. Mission fields in what became the United States were a polyglot of every Protestant denomination plus some Catholic activity.

9. McFague, *New Climate for Theology*, 47.

and cognizant of our own shortsightedness. It pushes us to understand that we exist in a network of relatedness. We should understand that we are not living in isolation but in a community with others who are affected by us.[10] Understanding these things will help us be loving towards each other and for each other.

First Plane Ride

I remember the day that my family and I immigrated to Canada. Clear as yesterday, I call to mind the anxiety and excitement that filled my stomach as we ventured into a foreign abyss to begin our new lives. I was five and my sister was six. We sold or gave away all of our belongings before our departure. Our whole lives were whittled down to a pile of small red bags. Our father had left a few months earlier, so it was just us three women; my mother, my sister, and I, who boldly confronted this new chapter of our lives clutching onto the only remnants of the past.

At the time, my paternal grandmother, who had never been on a plane, kept lecturing me and my older sister that there would be no bathrooms onboard. So we were careful not to drink any fluids and were ordered to go to the bathroom numerous times in anticipation of boarding. In the bathroom, my grandmother saw the juice I was carrying in my hand and emptied the bottle into the sink as she held a gaze with me in the reflection of the mirror. I could feel her about to erupt and start scolding me again, but I ran out of the bathroom before she got the chance. If this was what it was like to travel to new places, to be so hesitant and scared the whole time, then I didn't want anything to do with it.

But much to my amusement, once we boarded, I saw that there was indeed a bathroom—two in fact—and I looked back at my grandmother with a pleased look, thinking, "See, everything will be just fine." Now, when I think back to the frivolousness of it all, I realize that she was hyper anxious about our departure. We were all so young: me, my sister, even my mother. We didn't know what to expect. How could we?

We left Korea in 1975. At that time, there were no direct flights from Korea to Canada. We took a flight from Seoul to Hawaii, had an eight-hour layover, and then flew to Anchorage, Alaska. We had another long layover

---

10. To be fair, the kind of individualism growing out of some American denominations is non-biblical. There are ample passages in the New Testament that stress a community of humans as the body of Christ.

in Anchorage before finally arriving in Toronto. It was as if a whole year had passed before we ever set foot in our new home.

Times have changed. Since then, as travel has become more accessible, international travel has become much more popular. Now, there are countless direct flights from North America to Korea. Many people today move around for work, and these transient or nomadic people have become a modern phenomenon. Here in America, cultures have both conflicted with one another and coalesced, as people from all over the world come to pursue the American dream and make a new home.

In this age of global travel, it is essential that we open ourselves up to each other's histories, cultures, religions, and beliefs. When we do this, we become more cognizant of our commonalities rather than lingering on our differences. A part of this global movement is recognizing ourselves in those who are different from us. Discovering our similarities will allow us to build common ground. Such discovery will positively influence how we live in this world with one another and how we view the Spirit.

When the Church First Abandoned the Spirit

A few things happened to dampen the liveliness of the Spirit early on. Firstly, the church started to expand and develop into various parts of the empire. With new growth comes a myriad of internal problems, namely, disharmony within the church. The attempt to maintain the unity of belief across the quickly expanding church was vexing. What the church established as its ideologies had to be based on precedented beliefs, reckoned early on by its leaders. Consequently, these leaders fought any heresy that they believed was creeping into their ideology. Once a heresy emerged, it was usually debated and cleared up. One such example is the Arian controversy.

The early church was struggling with doctrine. The concern for orthodoxy would not allow a liberal movement of the Spirit to adapt and grow within the church. Jesus' disciples did not see the anticipated return of their master. Since Jesus was not returning, they tried to remember his teachings and scrambled to remember all that he had said. As they were sharing the good news, they also began to recognize the difficulties in resolving the humanity and divinity of Jesus. They made every effort to clearly and simply state who he was, but this difficulty endured for many generations.

There were two opposing camps surrounding the debate on the identity of Jesus: Athanasius believed Jesus to be *homoousios* (of one substance) with God, and Arius believed Jesus to be *homoiousios* (of similar substance) with God. During this controversy, Arius had a significantly larger following than Athanasius, resulting in a stronger following for Arius's line of thinking.

But to many, Arius's perspective appeared to posit two gods, and that was not acceptable in the fiercely monotheistic early church. It is difficult to equate Jesus with God when Jesus was human and fleshly. If he was divine, then Christianity appeared to be a polytheistic religion. Arius soon became associated with the phrase, "There was a time when he was not." Arius believed that Jesus could not have been of the same substance as God, for Jesus was created and not always with God. Since Jesus was created, he was a creature, thus leading to the conclusion that there must have been a time when he did not exist. This debate grew to seriously challenge the fragile unity of the early church.

The leaders of the church argued about the meaning of these two Greek words, separated by a single letter. The debate surrounding this single iota divided the church from before the Council of Nicea (325 CE) until even after the Council of Constantinople (381 CE). It remained an internal conflict within the church; however, it did not divide the church. At the end of the Council of Nicaea, which was set up to discuss this key christological issue, it was decided that Arius was a heretic. It was declared that Jesus is of the same substance as God and has always existed with God. Jesus was neither a creature nor created, but he was a being that was fantastically composed of the same substance of God. This was settled, and ultimately, Arius's supporters were discredited.

This decision signified that Christianity was purely monotheistic. They established Jesus' divinity for the sake of doctrine. The next question that came to a head was the relationship between the Spirit and God; the "third person" of the Trinity had to be defined and understood. The church's understanding of the Spirit at that time was clearly defined, and it stayed stagnant throughout much of Christian history. It has remained a white, Eurocentric pneumatology, which has not responded to the challenges and changing contexts throughout religious and social history.

Being in Two Communities

The community of creation includes us as human beings. We tend to separate ourselves from creation. Sometimes, we separate ourselves from who we are in other ways as well, denying ourselves our full dimension.

In between the space of East Asian and Western cultural identity lies a hazy dimension that I find myself in.

One of the greatest challenges of growing up within this hybrid culture came with my attempts to reconcile the differences between the two and elucidate my perception of self. My parents tried to keep my identity as purely Korean as possible—though they encouraged the excellence of English from an early age—while friends at school facilitated the plight to become more Westernized. During my teen years, I went against my parents' desires and sought to become as white as possible. I tried not to eat Korean food—at least, I pretended not to enjoy it. I pretended not to understand spoken Korean, as I would shake my head at Koreans and tell them in English, "No Korean." The more I tried, however, the more I realized how stubborn culture can be.

After many failed attempts to become the white girl I fantasized about—the girl with the pale, straight hair and clear, light eyes—I would inevitably return to a reflection of myself with complete disappointment, even failure. After years of arguing with myself and struggling to minimize my Asianness, I finally succumbed to the realization that I had to accept the identity, the face, the food, and the culture that was honestly my own. Like it or not, I had to renew my identity and negotiate the differences between the two disparate cultures.

As I get older, my appreciation of my Korean heritage deepens. I become more appreciative of my early experiences of self-attempted Westernization, and in hindsight, I find humor in it. It offered the unique experience of cultural deciphering and the space to explore who I was and where I fit within the changing landscapes I lived through.

It was a character-building time. A time to learn to recognize that being a hybrid is a certain kind of advantage, one that presents various touchstones of connection. Through this, I was able to formulate new ways of being. Discovering hybridity is an exciting adventure. It shaped my journey of Christianity, allowing me to embrace a unique path of negotiation and renewal.

Memory Verses and the Apostles' Creed

I grew up in a Baptist church, where I had to memorize Bible verses. It is always good practice to memorize Bible verses, but it is even better when the church gives nicely wrapped snacks as a prized reward. It was difficult to memorize the verses every week, and of course there were some verses that were easier than others. Once in awhile, I got stuck memorizing difficult passages such as those from the books of Daniel and Revelation. But the delicious snacks—pre-packaged lunch baggies full of a child's favorite foods all jumbled together: chips, pretzels, and candy—made it much easier to stay motivated.

In addition to the Baptist church, I also went to another—the Korean Presbyterian church—which offered the "Bible Sword" game. On Sundays, I would participate in contests where we tested our memory of Bible verses, sang hymns, and rehearsed and memorized the Apostles' Creed. At the time, church was everything to me. It was the central hub of my social life and where I practiced the majority of my extracurricular activities. As a young girl at the time, I was in need of constant entertainment and stimulation, and my parents believed there was a no better—or cheaper—place to get it than in the church. For me, it was a second home, and it has always provided me with something to do, a place to be, throughout my life. Along with the myriad of little games, contests, and activities, there were other ventures that involved discussions of God in the Trinity. This was the hardest exercise that I did as a child growing up in the church.

Subordinating the Son to the Father remained a threatening heresy. For Orthodox theologians in the East, the Father served as that principle of unity, giving birth to the Son and breathing forth the Spirit. T. F. Torrance and others have pointed out that making the Father the foundation of the Trinity risks subordinationism, rendering Son and Spirit as less than in comparison to Father. This endangers the equality that is so valued as a characteristic of the Trinity.[11] Any understanding of the Trinity must argue that the three are equal.

To counter subordination, one had to think through Cappadocian personalism, which posits that any person derives identity from those with whom that person is in relation. The three persons of the Trinity mutually define one another's identities[12] and are mutually dependent on one

---

11. Torrance, *Trinitarian Faith*, 240.
12. Placher, *Triune God*, 141.

another. By the end of the fourth century, Christian theologians had generally agreed that the claims for divinity they applied to the Son ought to apply to the Holy Spirit as well.[13]

These debates were largely grounded on Greek philosophy, and they relied on these categories to debate, discuss, and learn about God. This continued into the Medieval period and through the Reformation. European influence has dominated all Western discourse about the nature of God and the Trinity for two millennia. Take the phrase, the "absolute dependence on God," coined by Friedrich Schleiermacher (1768–1834). It makes sense in a Eurocentric theology, but less so for African or Asian theologies.

For example, in Asia, where there is heavy influence and practice of Buddhism, one practices *emptying* rather than *dependence*. Schleiermacher's way of thinking does not resonate or appeal to this Asian ideology as effectively as it may for the European mind. Euro-theology has shaped and molded Christian thinking for the past two thousand years. It's difficult to shake off this kind of thinking or to allow different types of thinking to have any kind of prominence. Christian theology has too often been an exclusive club for white, male, European theologians, without the necessary inclusion of minority voices and representation.

That is, until a more modern theology began to emerge from the United States in the mid-1950s, when new, diverse voices began to moderate white Euro-theology. At first, it was still much of the same, as it was mainly white Europeans who immigrated into the United States and engaged in theology. However, with the influx of immigrants from Asia, South America, and other areas, it became clearer over time that a singular, white, Eurocentric theology had failed to consider the diverse experiences of God—just as it had become clear to feminist theologians during the second wave feminism movement in the 1960s. They recognized that the mainstream theology was not addressing their concerns or allowing women's voices to be included in the theological discourse. Their voices were not being heard, and there arose a need for them to incorporate and acknowledge feminist theology.

In the same way that people protect their homes to maintain power over their property, Eurocentric theology had also become protective of what it (wrongly) considered its "property." Different voices threatened to trespass into their collectivist idea of Christianity. To this day, white Eurocentric theology aims to present itself culturally as pristine, holy, and true. All other variations and perspectives are rendered dirty, evil, and untrue.

---

13. Placher, *Triune God*, 83.

They want to portray a negative perspective of syncretism and hybridity without admitting to the hybridity intrinsic to Old Testament theology, New Testament theology, and Euro-theology. If we hope to get any closer to an informed understanding of the Holy Spirit in this book, we're going to have to approach things differently; we are going to fuse, mix, and whisk things together, until a united blend of hybrid theology ultimately emerges.

Hybrid Theology

Our life is full of hybridity. The produce that we now consume is not what it once was less than a century ago, as things have been meticulously bred and cultivated into the familiar hybrids we now see at the grocery store. In popular culture, there are several films that follow the narratives of hybridity, particularly that of mixed people and hybrid identities. For instance, *Rabbit Proof Fence*, a film based on a true story, recalls the events of Aboriginal people in Australia, whose mixed children are taken away from their families and communities to be made "white" through forced marriages to white people. This endeavor was facilitated through a government program that aimed to phase out hybridity, breeding out the dark skin of Aboriginal peoples so they would become physically and culturally "whitened." By the third generation, they would, for all intents and purposes, be white. This devastating assimilation and attempt to eradicate a race of people eventually became less valuable to the white Australian, and finally this practice of phasing out hybridity was outlawed around 1969.[14]

Hybridity is an evolutionary process that molds and changes individuals and societies. It combines other ideas, concepts, and beliefs to come up with a new and different understanding of the self and the world. It lifts up the reality that we are not pure, pristine, and simplistic but rather beings of beautiful chaos, interdependence, and complexity. Hybridization is constantly occurring, which implies that new concepts and forms are always emerging.

We live in a mixed culture. It is essential, a fundamental state for housing social development and collective progression. However, hybridity is not simply mixing different languages or juxtaposing different cultures, as if the two lie on equal footing.[15] This image of cultures as simple entities of equality is false, as there will always be one culture that is more

---

14. Knightley, "Longtime Australian Policy."
15. Kwok, *Postcolonial Imagination and Feminist Theology*, 169.

long-standing, powerful, and dominant. Hybridity involves the creation of a new form, which can then be set against the old form, of which it is partly made.[16]

Hybridization fuses two things together, transforming them to produce a third, new entity.[17] Hybridity reinforces the notion that nothing remains static or permanent, as all things are in a constant state of change. Ideas and forms collide, and new concepts are formulated and produced.

Hybridity is not just a mosaic of cultures existing next to each other; it is an intermingling and interweaving of societies. Each culture mixes with others to produce new, distinct cultures from the juxtaposition of ideas, thoughts, and cultures. This alteration may not be welcomed or embraced by all groups, and in many cases, the dominant will resist change to negate the exposition and dispersion of their power. However, when power is shared, those who formerly held power will have to confront the inevitable change and consequence of being closer to equity. In truth, there is no culture that is not hybrid.

Hybridity is an effective tool to frame traditions. The Spirit of God became an object to be studied rather than a divine being. The church continues to debate the Spirit and what the Spirit is rather than allowing the Spirit to become and be who she is, just as YHWH stated in the burning bush, "I WILL BE WHO I WILL BE." Christians get wrapped up in orthodoxy, good practice, and the limits of the Spirit rather than letting the Spirit move freely.

We debate about the movement of the Spirit throughout the church's history. We debate this Spirit as if it were an object. If we do not treat it as an object, then it becomes something so fantastical that it is rendered as an entity beyond our mental comprehension. We see this in certain groups that live out the Spirit and pretend that the Spirit of God is in them and that it wants to move within their lives.

We have inherited a very philosophical understanding of the Holy Spirit, often limiting us from viewing it in any other way. Christianity has been so entrenched in the Western, white, Eurocentric theology that it has silenced all other voices around the globe. Furthermore, the Spirit has been too often ignored (except by Pentecostals), becoming a junior member of the Trinity rather than a full-fledged member.

---

16. Young, *Colonial Desire*, 22, 25.
17. Goldberg, "Heterogeneity and Hybridity," 80.

As we engage in hybrid theology, we must dig into the Bible to get a hybrid understanding of the Spirit to enlighten us for our contextual theology today. We cannot ignore contextual theology, which pushes us out of the limiting structures of white, Eurocentric theology. Rather, we must create a new safe space that will support the immigrants, refugees, queers, misfits, and the other.

Global Context

In an ever interconnected world, the demand to contextualize our means of communication in relation to the globalizing environment becomes ever more important. The world is becoming smaller, and communities are becoming more malleable to the shifts of cultural integration. Within my own city, I have been a witness to the progressive changes in cultural attitudes as white Americans, African Americans, Hispanics, and Asians unionize—whether it be for the birth of new families or the fortification of the economic landscape.

The direction we are headed is positive, but we cannot ignore the fragmented and socially disparate state that the US has been historically enveloped in. There is still a need to educate ourselves about those cultures and religions with which we are unfamiliar. The fear that is harbored in our country regarding *the other* remains alive and strong, a reality that must be acknowledged and actively addressed. We should embrace them. If we wish not just to survive, but to *live* in peace, we need to love and welcome those who are different.

Another crucial dimension to the subject of the globalizing world, in addition to how we humans socialize with one another, is how we interact with our own environment. It is not just humans we should be concerned with. We live in constant ignorance of the rapidly changing biosphere and environmental behaviors in which we engage. We live carelessly, raping the Earth as we exploit all of its resources. We have polluted the land, air, and water so severely that finding them in healthy and clean conditions is becoming increasingly more rare and now commodified. As one industrial power improves its environment, new industrial countries evolve to produce worse pollution.

In recent times, we have discovered countless instances of environmental abuse, many of them covert and hidden from the public. Major private corporations partner with those in power—the wealthy, politicians, and government workers—and push unethical agendas. I believe this to be one of the most significant issues in American politics, as innumerable instances of this abuse of power go unreported, without coverage in the mainstream media, thus excluded from public awareness.

One of the most significant recent examples of this is the ongoing water crisis in Flint, Michigan, where their citizens suffer from contaminated water sources. It has exposed over 100,000 residents to elevated lead levels, and it is still unresolved.

The lack of safe drinking water is not limited to third world countries, like many people believe; it is happening right here in our home country. We need to demand international and global partnering to improve the environmental state of our communities and the larger marine and terrestrial biomes on which our lives depend.

We must be conscious in how we choose to live today. If we can learn to live with strangers, with those who differ from us, with the creatures of the animal kingdom, and with our planet Earth, we can save ourselves and protect future generations that will be faced with the damage we have done. It is crucial that we be open to the Spirit and allow it to live within us and move us. With the work and movement of the Spirit, we can live out the gospel justly, and with the love of God in our hearts, we can be privy to the effects of the ever-present Spirit.

I examine the Spirit as *chi*, as light, wind, breath, and vibration. As we reimagine the Spirit in this way, we will begin to understand how this can help us cope and bear some of the pain and suffering that we experience in this world. Koreans call unjust suffering *han*. *Han* is the debilitation and disruption of one's life. It is important to release this *han* so that it doesn't inflict more damage on one's own spiritual and physical life. It is the Spirit who helps heal the pain of *han*.

As we explore the Holy Spirit, we recognize how the Spirit impacts every aspect of our lives. In many ways, the Spirit tends to be ignored. We must reclaim the importance and the power of the Spirit. We must welcome the Spirit into our lives and allow the Spirit to bring healing to us, to each other, and to the Earth. We as Christians need to come together to eliminate injustices and work towards a more peaceful reign of God.

Han

Han is a Korean word for the feelings and experiences of unjust suffering. Discriminatory biases, such as racism, sexism, classism, and colonialism, all create *han*. The pain is more intense and less amenable to relief if such dispositions are built into the political system. Such systems inflict suffering upon entire classes, generations, and communities.

In possessing more than others without sharing generously, we are committing a sin and creating *han*. Keeping resources we do not need, while others labor and struggle to survive, has become a part of the American capitalist culture and an integral effect of the American Dream. Christians talk a lot about sin; indeed, we are all sinners in need of redemption. We have a tendency to concentrate on this vertical relationship that refers to God and us, often at the expense of our horizontal relationships, those between us and our neighbors. Neglecting horizontal relationships results in harmful acts against our neighbors and the environment. *Han* reminds us of our horizontal relationships.[18]

Our bonds with others and with nature are extremely important. We cannot neglect these connections as God commanded all of us to love with the whole of our heart, soul, mind, and strength to support our neighbors and ultimately ourselves. One way to emphasize the horizontal relationship is to recognize the *han* we cause others as we indulge in gluttony, greed, and lust, oblivious to the injustice it creates within our global economy.

Han is the wrong deed committed against another person and the pain that ensues. It is the unjust suffering and sorrow of being sinned against. We in Western society are sinning against others as we live a bountiful but self-indulgent lifestyle because we turn a blind eye to those beyond our borders. Justice and morality, like our laws, end at the water's edge. When the rest of the world looks at us, they see themselves as victims of our sin, whose only hope seems to be to regain power through conflict.[19]

Han is the painful rupture of one's soul caused by abuse, exploitation, injustice, and violence. The hurt soul is a pollutive one. When the aching soul is wounded again by external violence, the victim suffers a deeper ache, often perpetuating their pain by passing it on to others.[20]

---

18. Kim, *Colonialism, Han, and the Transformative Spirit*, 49.
19. Kim, *Colonialism, Han, and the Transformative Spirit*, 49.
20. Park, *From Hurt to Healing*, 11–12.

This damage can be attributed to countless things, but in our society it is very often inflicted by a capitalist mindset that focuses on personal gain with an unempathetic, calculated method of control to increase profit. Here is the most fertile ground for the growing self-serving that capitalism demands. This work is an end in itself, a "calling" one might even say.[21]

Han captures wrong deeds that we do to one another, often by breaking promises, treaties, and confidences. It captures the feeling of being sinned against. As inhabitants of a privileged society, we must acknowledge the reality that others lose from our capital gain. When those outside of the Western world look at us, they see that underneath the surface of material prosperity is profound greed, deception, and sin.[22]

Han is the theological motif that can be used to help us understand the current condition of our world. *Han* describes the depths of human suffering as one sins against another. *Han* also denotes repressed feelings of suffering through oppression from others, natural calamities, or illness. For example, the atrocities that Japan committed in China during the Second World War fed China's repressed hatred towards the Japanese, which further compounded earlier atrocities committed against them. We have seen this hatred break out several times in the two nations' territorial disputes.

Likewise, in more recent times, active hatred arises as treachery is cloaked in the ego-driven game of international business. For example, when a large corporation moves a plant from now-wealthy Ireland to starving Madagascar, there is no local manager to whom one may appeal any grievances or issues at the plant. *Han* captures this wrong. Theologian Andrew Sung Park states that *han* can be defined as the critical wound of the heart generated by unjust psychosomatic repression as well as social, political, economic, and cultural oppression. It is entrenched in the hearts of victims of sin and violence and is expressed through a breadth of negative reactions such as sadness, helplessness, hopelessness, resentment, hatred, and the will to seek revenge.[23]

Beyond our own human *han* is the *han* of animals and nature. God placed human beings as stewards over the Earth and the Earth's other living inhabitants; yet animals and nature suffer increasingly from abusive treatment by humans, which goes uncontested as they cannot protest it for themselves. *Han* is their inexpressible pain of being maltreated. Creation

---

21. Weber, *Protestant Ethic*, 18.
22. Kim, *Colonialism, Han, and the Transformative Spirit*, 51.
23. Park, *Wounded Heart of God*, 10.

was not meant to be subjected to sinful human exploitation. It is being forced to serve human whims and has suffered the pain in silence. Nature tries to cope with all the stress it receives, but it is not always able to bear that stress. Eventually, it collapses under the weight; this is *han*.[24]

We can still prevent this from happening. Good stewardship brings an awareness of the injustices caused to humanity and nature, requiring us Christians to take responsibility for it. Stewardship asks us to be accountable for our actions and their consequences. We need to decide. How much are we going to allow our actions to be dictated by society's consumerist inclinations? How are we going to deal with our *han* and its effects on the *han* of the Earth?[25]

Korea

To understand the concept of *han*, one must understand the history of Korea, and to do that, one must understand Korea's geography. Korea sits on a peninsula that abuts China, with Japan lying east across the sea. In some ways, it is similar to Israel, sandwiched between two major Asiatic powers in the nineteenth and twentieth centuries. Strategically, being a peninsula presents Korea with unique security problems.[26] When an enemy invades, there is nowhere to run. It is like being between France and England when they were in a long global dispute with one another in the eighteenth and nineteenth centuries. The people can resist the invader, but should the invader prove stronger, defeat inevitably follows.

Throughout much of its history, the small, hermit kingdom of Korea was united. Division came only at the end of the Second World War. However, the unified Korea endured colonialism and domination from Japan as a result of the Sino-Japanese and Russo-Japanese wars in the nineteenth and twentieth centuries. Korea became part of the Japanese Empire in 1910. Though Koreans did not like to travel and generally kept to themselves, the neighboring countries of China and Japan invaded Korea often, as its scale and power was easy to dominate. Such trauma has had a legacy on

---

24. Park, *Wounded Heart of God*, 42.

25. Kim, *Colonialism, Han, and the Transformative Spirit*, 53.

26. This was amply demonstrated during the Korean conflict, when the North Korean army drove South Korean and UN forces south to Pusan, coming close to pushing them into the sea. The flip side of the peninsular disadvantages was the UN landing at Inchon, cutting off the North Koreans by amphibious assaults.

the Korean mindset, shaping the cultural and social standards that prevail today.

As a kid, I had a lot of cavities. So naturally, one of my least favorite places to visit, like many other children, was the dentist's office. I was the "super-careful-brush-your-teeth-after-every-meal" and "don't-eat-too-much-candy-as-it-will-cause-cavities" kind of girl. I was careful to drink water over juice or soda and limit acid and sugar, pushing my obsessive tendencies towards those around me. With all this careful oral hygiene, I was nevertheless still faced with a barrage of cavities and dentist visits.

Getting my teeth fixed was traumatic: the dentist had his assistants hold me down as I squirmed in fear, pulling my mouth open while he injected multiple needles into my gums and drilled deep holes into my teeth. Each time, I would enter with sweaty palms, a racing heart, and an intense head rush.

If the dentist was the height of my physical pain and discomfort, then Korean school was the height of my emotional pain. I approached Korean school the exact same way as I did when I went to the dentist's office—kicking and screaming. I would throw major tantrums, forcing my parents to physically drag me as I exploded in a frenzy. As irony would have it, I now find myself dragging my children, kicking and screaming, to Korean school. My youngest always says that going to Korean school will be the "death of him." I can understand his feelings, having gone through those same swings of emotion those many years ago.

Simply put, I didn't like Korean school because it was difficult. The sentence structure of the Korean language is the opposite of English, so I was understandably confused by both languages I had to practice. I had to learn English at school and then flip the lingual composition afterwards at Korean school. But it wasn't just a language barrier. In Korean language school, every teacher I had would draw the map of Korea and tell us how it looked like a rabbit's profile. Each time the teacher repeated this action, I would scoff, rolling my eyes and asking myself, "Why do they have to remind me every time they draw the map of Korea?" I was sick of the monotony.

Yet that repeated image of Korea's map started to manifest in my mind the more I saw it. The resemblance never left me. I am always reminded of this frivolous comparison when I think about Korea's history. Vulnerable to being hunted by predatory animals and humans—for consumption, fur usage, or a lucky rabbit foot charm—the rabbit has often been referenced for its position as meek prey.

As a small, historically repressed, and economically weak country, Korea, up until recent times, has shared much resemblance to the victimized rabbit. In its traumatic history, it has been dominated or "hunted" by neighboring countries and incessantly invaded by more powerful colonies. If China did not invade Korea, then Japan did, and if Japan did not invade, then China did. Korea was the rabbit for these hunters.

Numerous invasions harmed the Korean national identity as well as its citizens. The country and its people have felt unjustly torn by mightier forces far beyond their ability to combat. This colonization and domination strongly impacted the country, shaping the Korean people and their culture into what we know today.

A Comfort Woman's Story

In the fall of 1994, I had the privilege of listening to a surviving "comfort woman" speak about her experiences during World War II. She spoke at an event held by Toronto's Korean Cultural Center to honor and remember the women who suffered against the mass abuse and violation of power during this period. Before she came out to speak about her experiences, female religious leaders gave an invocation, led a prayer, and did responsive reading. Then, a small, elderly woman came out to speak. As I watched this tiny frail woman emerge, I was shocked when I was confronted by her force of energy. She spoke with such tenacity, capturing the emotions of the crowded audience and reporters with her presence alone.

Before becoming a comfort woman, she was just a girl. She recounted how she was kidnapped by Japanese men from her home and taken out of Korea. She did not know where she was being taken, but she knew from the duration of the journey that she was far from home. Once she arrived to this unknown destination, she was bound up and locked alone in a small, dark room.

The first night she was there, the door opened startlingly. A man came in—a high-ranking Japanese general—who grimly muttered something to her and proceeded to rip off all her clothes. He forced himself onto her, violently raping her as she capsized in fear, until she soon fainted afterwards. When she finally woke up, she found herself naked and covered in blood. She said the generals were the first to rape "new" girls as they were disease free. After the other high-ranking officers raped them, the soldiers had their turn. During this time, she was violated fifty to seventy times a night. She was filled with immense *han* and continued to live in this hell with no hope of getting out.

Most of the comfort women died of illness, while many soldiers killed those who became pregnant or who contracted too many diseases. This woman remembered one day when the soldiers took countless comfort women outside to witness a killing. The soldiers announced to the women that one of the comfort women was too diseased to live. So their solution was to rip off her clothes; then, one of the soldiers brought out a gun, and motioned her to come over. The soldier then put the gun up her vagina and pulled the trigger.

After spending years as a comfort woman for Japanese men, our speaker was finally freed when the Japanese were defeated in 1945. The few surviving women woke up one morning and saw that all the soldiers were gone. They huddled together and left the compound with their bodies broken and souls shattered. As they walked away from the compound, they were overwhelmed with sadness, bewilderment, fear, and anguish. The emotional and physical damage was unfathomable. As past comfort women, these women lived with the enduring shame of what happened to them. Most did not return home to their families, and as a result harbored a dark and strong *han* for the rest of their lives. Nearly all lived in isolation, without getting married or having families of their own.

This courageous woman said that she would continue to tell her story until the world understood the atrocities that happened to these young women. At the end of her talk, the room fell silent. We looked around at each other in shock, meeting shining eyes of complete commiseration.

She finally said, again and again, that she would die in *han*.

Han in Confucian Culture

Akin to many other major societies across the world, women in Korea are subject to the strong patriarchy that can be manipulatively interpreted through Confucianism. Confucianism is a way of life that began with Confucius in the sixth to fifth century BCE. It is a worldview and way of life that is embedded in patriarchy. Confucianism teaches that a woman is to obey her father when young, her husband when she is married, and her son when she is widowed.

While men are given the freedom of behavior, beliefs, and expression, women are far more limited in such capacities, relegated to the societal institutions of family and home. I saw this within my own family, as my paternal and maternal grandmothers grew up within this society. This level of patriarchy was overt and conspicuous. I remember both of them using *han* to talk about their experiences.

My paternal grandmother's close friend suffered abuse throughout her life. Her husband psychologically abused her, often threatening to kill her. He would hurl heavy clay bowls at her head and chase her around the house with a kitchen knife. She would often leave these episodes of assault with broken bones, black eyes, and incapacitating migraines from the fear and anxiety she suffered. Yet she held in the pain. Like other sufferers of abuse, she was too ashamed to report the horrific abuse. In Korea, which is a honor/shame society, many abused women do not want to reveal their pains, rarely reporting domestic accounts of abuse to save face. As a result, she did not ever escape her husband's violence, and it continued to occur up until his very death.

The *han* she bore was heavy. The constant threat of death in her tiny apartment complex debilitated her, and the pain of seeing her children living in the same fear compounded her *han*. When her husband came home or was in the home, her kids would often hide themselves in the closet, afraid of being attacked. She endured this incessant abuse silently. She is not alone. Countless women suffer just like her.

In Korea, husbands call their wives "*an nae*," which is literally translated as "inside." Women were understood and expected to stay inside, within the home: cooking, cleaning, raising children, and tending to their husbands. Outside, they did not belong—as that was a man's world.

Korean women possess great amounts of *han*. We are emotional and expressive people, so you will often hear Korean women say, "*han e mae chul*," meaning that they have so much *han* that they will die with it. Unquestionably, such unreleased *han* is not exclusive to Korea, as it exists within every parameter of the world. We need to seek ways of releasing this pain and moving towards fortifying the soul.

Han in North America

Unfixed to a place, time, or person, *han* is experienced by all peoples. Within a North American context, an immigrant of non-European descent coming into America may be viewed with alienation and fear. For instance, the Muslim community within our country is portrayed in a heavily negative light and spoken through bigoted discourse. They are painted as radicals, savages, and terrorists. Hispanics are often viewed as illegal immigrants, "conniving" individuals who come to America seeking new life, escaping economic limitations without legal papers and documentation. Additionally, Asian Americans are long held as the minority role model, the perpetual foreigners. Asian Americans are viewed as unsocialized, skilled, studious workers at the detriment of other people of color. The myth of being a model minority pits Asian Americans against other people of color, causing further tension and problems between all people of color. In addition, the lack of fair media representation has also led to Asian Americans still being viewed as outsiders.

In my own Asian American experience, I have seen how we often serve as scapegoats for economic problems. For example, in periods of rising unemployment, white Americans have blamed Asian Americans for "stealing" their jobs and possessing coveted spaces in higher education. For instance, we can look towards the case of Vincent Chin,[27] a young man who was beaten to death by two white men who believed they lost their jobs due to the rapidly increasing sales of Japanese cars. However, Vincent Chin was Chinese American and not Japanese American. Subsequent to his death, his murderers accepted a plea bargain and received minimal fines and probation. For whatever problems that may arise, Asians are often easy targets for their economic prosperity and proliferation into educational institutions and corporate workforces.

The experience of racism can be deadly. We look towards the lives that have recently been lost as a preventable outcome of prejudice. Trayvon Martin,[28] a seventeen-year-old, was wrongfully targeted by a neighborhood watch and fatally shot in Stanford, Florida. Because he was a young, black male wearing a black hoodie, he posed a dangerous threat to the mind of his fearful and ignorant killer. Michael Brown was a black teenage boy who was shot by a white police officer in Ferguson, Missouri. He was suspected of potential robbery or jaywalking and was shot dead, despite being unarmed. Walter Scott, another unarmed black man, was shot by a white police officer as he was running away. There appeared to be no actual threat or reason to warrant his deadly force. After the endless successive murders of African

27. Wang, "Who is Vincent Chin?"
28. Botelho, "What Happened."

Americans by government authorities, the "BlackLivesMatter" movement emerged in 2013. This is the black community's response to their suffering of *han*.

Middle Eastern or Arab-looking Muslims experiences of discrimination leads them to experience *han*. When white people commit violent crimes, their actions are viewed as those of individuals; their actions are often explained as being rooted in mental illness, personal trauma, or anger. Yet when Muslims commit violent crimes, they are labeled as "terrorists" and "radicals," further elevating their crimes to a new level of unmanageable human evil and condemnation.

Non-white suspects are regularly viewed differently by the public and treated inequitably by the police, government officials, and the criminal justice system. This burden creates *han* for the individuals who experience the racism firsthand as well as for the communities to which they belong.

In addition to racism, the sexism we experience in North America adds to the *han* of many women and men. Countless young girls are taken to work as domestic slaves in foreign countries or are manipulated into being victims of sex trafficking. The 2014 Global Slavery Index (GSI) found that there are 36 million victims of human trafficking worldwide. Nearly two-thirds of the people who are trafficked come from Asia.[29] Their identification documents are taken to make it difficult for them to return to their home country. Barriers are quickly established to keep them as slaves while their traffickers profit. These young women experience unbelievable circumstances, and live through the trauma of abuse, exploitation, torture, rape, and physiological terror. *Han* pierces their hearts and generates animosity, hatred, and resentment towards others.

My Own *Han*

Growing up in Canada, I faced my share of racism and sexism. While working on my PhD at the University of Toronto, I had many Asian, male classmates. Several of them told me on multiple occasions that I had a greater obligation to stay home and have children than to pursue my degree. I remember one male student in particular remarked, "God will be more pleased if you have one child than ten PhD degrees."

The pressure to fit into their idealistic mold of an Asian woman was a lot to carry. It was not just my colleagues who expressed these ideas but also

---

29. Enos, "Nearly Two-Thirds of Human Trafficking."

many of my closest family members and friends, whose opinions I regarded highly. It seemed wherever I went, some patriarchal Korean doctoral student would tell me to stop studying and to become a domestic caretaker instead. It was burdensome, especially when I was made to feel unwelcome at lunch circles or other social gatherings.

I was married around the same time as most of my friends, so naturally they had kids around the same time as well. But as I became deeper enveloped in academia, I grew to be more disparate. To those around me, I was somewhat of an oddball, a married Korean woman, approaching her thirties, who spent her days at the library studying rather than being at home with her kids and husband. I could not shake off the feeling that I was disappointing people around me, and the gratified attitude I tried to maintain started to falter and eventually withered. I felt out of the loop, too far from the life stage I was expected to be in. So staying home to have children as I worked on my degree became a reality.

I had my first son, Theodore, in the midst of working on my comprehensive exams. But the patriarchal burden did not leave me even then. My peers, family, and friends would continue to tell me to stay home and care for my son and try to give him a sibling. Those around me came to define my life as I became more responsive to their ideas of what I should be doing. My in-laws were furious, shocked that their daughter-in-law was studying rather than staying home and taking care of her baby. They pressured me to drop out of my PhD program and do what was right "by the family" by becoming a stay-at-home mom. But the reality was that I was doing both. I was taking care of my baby as well as studying. It was extremely difficult to maintain a healthy work-life balance, and eventually, the pressure and the stress took a severe toll; I lost wellness in my health, my studies, my mind, and my life.

I became physically weak, feeling constant head rushes and numbness in my legs from trying to stand up. I broke out in hives all over my body. My immune system started to break down; I contracted one infection after another. I was nearing a psychological breakdown and went to see multiple therapists and counselors to help me cope with the mental strain. I was worried about how my condition would affect those around me, especially my baby. For me, this was *han* in every sense of the word. Individuals from this systemic, patriarchal, and Confucian cultural background sought to prevent me from reaching my goals. Barriers within family, the classroom, and my cultural community caused enormous *han,* and it continued to break me and my body down. Eventually, healing came as I dealt with the issue of *han* head on, ultimately proving my critics wrong as I became a successful academic and mother.

As we continue to reflect on pain, suffering, and *han*, the next chapter will examine the Spirit as light, and how it illuminates some of the problems that humanity has created to perpetuate more *han* in our world.

CHAPTER 2

Spirit as Light

THE BIBLE SPEAKS OF the Spirit as light. We see numerous illustrations of this imagery throughout Christian history and Christian theology. Despite Scripture's identification of the Spirit with light, the presence and significance of this identification has often been neglected, it's profound ambiguity often leading to a lack of understanding. Generally, the discourse in connection to the Spirit has reflected Christianity's tendency to focus on Jesus. As Christianity tries to center its attention on the Trinity and attempts to bring the Spirit back, it becomes increasingly necessary that we acknowledge how we experience the Spirit and how the Spirit is presented in the Scriptures and perceived in the church.

Light in the World

Light is essential for nearly all living beings on Earth. By nature, plants require light to grow and survive; larger, organic life forms sustain themselves in a complex ecosystem that is dependent on plant life; and humanity, imposed at the top of such a system, depends upon everything within this structure. We all need light to live, and the Earth needs it to survive. In Genesis, God created light, and that light gave forth new life. Light is a form of energy that makes it possible for us to see, to perceive life around us in vivid color and clarity.

The sun is the source of life-giving light. That energy becomes visible to us when it reaches a certain wavelength, around 380 to 400 nanometers. There are longer wavelengths of light, referred to as infrared light, and shorter wavelengths of light, called ultraviolet light. Most species of plants

Spirit as Light

welcome both infrared and ultraviolet light, and some animals are even able to discern it, while humans have only been privy to this light in recent times, through advancing technology. Infrared light is a form of invisible energy that can be felt through heat, and all objects in the universe emit some levels of it.

While some forms of light are undetected by the human eye and others are perceptually illuminating, its formidable effects can also be blinding. Perhaps it is most familiar in day-to-day life, when the blinds are drawn in the morning and you momentarily see a wash of clear, stark brightness. Or even as children, looking directly into the sun as a self-testing practice, only to realize that your vision gets impaired afterwards. It has the power to give us sight, and it also has the power to take it away.

Exposure to sunlight gives us pleasure, but more often than not, it can be immensely damaging; it dehydrates us, burns our skin, generates skin cancers, and even causes our photo memorabilia to fade into bleached obscurity.

While the brightest light, daylight, comes from the sun, light can also be seen in the shadows of the night. In the darkness, we can see fireflies, fires, stars, candles, torches, light from our electric light bulbs, and moonlight—a mere reflection of the sun's light. There is also light at dawn and at twilight. At dawn, we are able to see the first light of the day before sunrise. Lighting up the sky when the night is beginning, the sun is below the horizon and the refracted rays are bent by the atmosphere, providing another kind of illumination, twilight.

In a dark world, we depend on light for guidance: a bedside table lamp for late night clarity as we get ready for bed, lighthouses for guiding ships, and street lamps that illuminate the roads and sidewalks. Light has always been able to guide us in the outside physical world, but it also gives direction within our inner spiritual world. We use the image of light to talk about spiritual illumination, inner light, enlightenment, or the truth. We say that light helps us in times of hardship and in times of emotional darkness. We speak of the warm light that shows us the way out of the darkness of pain.

As we discuss these outer and inner worlds, we can identify that it is the Holy Spirit that is the light. In our present context, we face a societal darkness that has begun to take hold in overwhelmingly powerful ways. Climate change, war, racial and gender inequality, abuse of power, political corruption—the list goes on. It is easy to ruminate on the world's problems and get lost in the noise, but we must be proactive, and we must work toward building solutions rather than simply disputing around the issue at hand. We do not solely rely on ourselves but also on the Spirit as we seek solutions to these problems. The Spirit as light can clarify and shed light on these important issues, giving us direction and greater purpose.

Light in Creation

In the Genesis 1 creation story, God created the light first, and the light gave forth life. In Genesis, light is created on the first day and also the fourth day. The two divergent lights created on two different days can be confusing to readers, leaving them to wonder what the difference is between the light created on the first day the light created on the fourth day.

In Genesis 1:3–5 the word for "light" is a general, all-purpose Hebrew word for light, אור (occurs 176 times in the Hebrew Bible). The key in these verses is that God "separates" (הבדיל) "light" (אור) from "darkness" (חשׁך) (v. 4). So on the first day, there appears to be a clear distinction being made between light and darkness.[1]

In Genesis 1:14–16 the word for light is מאור, which is seldom used in Scripture (this word only occurs 19 times in the Hebrew Bible). This word still basically means "light." The purpose of these greater and lesser lights is to "give light" upon the Earth (v. 15). This is the verbal form of the noun אור used in vv. 3–5. But they also serve the same purpose as in vv. 3–5 to "separate" (הבדיל) "light" (אור) from "darkness" (חשׁך).

God offers the light for all of us to live. God's light lives within us and aids us in our creative work. Creation is ongoing as God gives us God's light that is the Spirit. We are to become co-creators with God and allow this Earth to become a place to sustain life. When God creates us, a part of God's light comes within us. The Spirit of God dwells within all of us. It gives us the inner strength to move ahead and co-create with God. We are to be the creative directors in our lives, helping to sustain the world and not destroy it.

---

1. This discussion on light in Genesis arose out of a personal discussion with Dr. Nancy Bowen in the Fall of 2018.

Spirit as Light

Jesus as Light

The Bible speaks of Spirit as light, offering text and imagery that depict the Spirit as light in Christianity. Light, being an edifying guide in our life, guides not only our outside physical world but also our inner spiritual world and its direction. We need light to help us in times of hardship and emotional wear.

Jesus says, "I am the light of the world. Whoever follows me will never walk in darkness but will have the light of life" (John 8:12). The Light and the Spirit are binary partners, bringing their source of goodness into the world. The light becomes the divine presence in our lives. We encounter the light directly, often finding the light within us. The light of Christ is the inner light. It is Christ's work in the human heart (John 1:9).

Jesus tells his disciples before his death that he will send a comforter and an advocate: "I will ask the Father, and he will give you another Advocate to be with you forever" (John 14:16). Here, the apostles were celebrating the Jewish harvest festival, called Shavuot, when the Holy Spirit descended upon them. Pentecost is fifty days after Passover and is the day of the first harvest of the season (Num 28:26). People gathered in Jerusalem to celebrate this Jewish holiday.[2] On that particular day, the Spirit sounded like a strong wind and looked like tongues of fire. The Spirit as light descended upon those at Pentecost and without fluctuation continues to come down upon us today.

It is God's plan that believers become more like Christ every day. "You are all children of the light and children of the day. We do not belong to the night or to the darkness" (1 Thess 5:5). God is the Creator of light as well as the giver of spiritual light, by which we can see the truth. Light exposes that which is hidden in darkness; it shows things as they really are. To walk in the light means to know God, understand the truth, and live in righteousness.

We see other biblical images of the Spirit as light. On the road to Damascus, Saul encountered Christ, who came to him as a blinding light and a voice. The light spoke out, "Why are you persecuting me?" The Spirit as light transformed Saul from the persecutor of the followers of Jesus to a faithful witness to Jesus. To signify his transformation by the divine Spirit, Saul changed his name to Paul.

---

2. Chase, *New Testament Study Guide*, 171.

Reimagining Spirit

While light is referenced in Scripture and historical texts, we can also find it referenced throughout art and contemporary pop culture. For example, the song, "Turn on Your Love Light," by The Grateful Dead:

> Without a warning you broke my heart, takin' it baby, tore it apart,
> And you left me standin' in the dark, said your love for me was dyin',
> Come on baby, baby please come on baby, cause I'm on my knees,
> Turn on your lights, let it shine on me, shine on your love light.

The light shows us the way of repenting our sin and living out the gospel. Moving towards the light means walking with Christ. Moving towards the light means living out the Sermon on the Mount. The Sermon on the Mount serves as a guide to help us live our lives based on the gospel, teaches us the value and meaning of being filled with the Spirit and the light, and describes the life that Jesus invites us to build here on Earth.

God as Light

By allowing God's light to shine in our lives, we come to see that Jesus is the "true light."[3] Jesus and Spirit are closely associated in the Trinity, and their connection is undeniable when it comes to pneumatology.

As we reflect on the Trinity and see that Jesus is God, we can come to recognize the numerous biblical references that describe God as light. 1 John 1:5 says, "God is light; in him there is no darkness at all." Note that we are not told that God is a light but rather that God is light. Light is part of God's essence, as is love (1 John 4:8). Jesus described himself as light: "I am the light of the world. Whoever follows me will never walk in darkness but will have the light of life" (John 8:12). Jesus also used light as an image of living for his followers: "Let your light shine before others, that they may see your good deeds" (Matt 5:16). We all have the light within us, and we need to bear the light for the world to see.

The Spirit of God means the presence of God. It is the *Shekinah*,[4] the Spirit of God which is within us. To live lives filled with hope and peace,

---

3. "The true light, which enlightens everyone, was coming into the world" (John 1:9).

4. The Shekhina(h) (also spelled Shekina[h], Schechina[h], or Shechina[h]; Biblical Hebrew: שכינה) is the English transliteration of a Hebrew word meaning "dwelling" or "settling" and denotes the dwelling or settling of the divine presence of God. The Shekhinah is the feminine aspect of Divinity, also referred to as the Divine Presence. See Columbia University Press, "Shekinah."

we seek to experience God every day, to be in God's presence. Psalm 4:6 says, "Let the light of your face shine on us, O Lord!" We can let this psalm be our prayer for God's presence/Light/Spirit to be within us and to shine through us. The Light makes us grow stronger as it gives us power within. The Light is one of the strongest properties in the world. It has the capacity to break night's darkness, and it can break through the darkest part of our lives to give hope, sustenance, and love.

In times of darkness, the absence of light may fill the emptiness in our lives. We walk through the valley of the shadow of death, where we face our own demons: past pains, present ones, illness, or even our own mortality. We will face many dark periods, yet in our darkness, God's light shines upon us, giving us love, mercy, and peace. It gives us the power to face the evil that comes our way.

God is Spirit, but God is also the Word. Traditionally, God has been understood as masculine, so terms such as *Word* were often used to talk about God. Word is *logos* in Greek, and it is masculine. God as logos is the reason that empowers us with God's transformative justice to move the world towards a more peaceful and loving community.

Acknowledging God's wondrous presence requires us to act justly with all of creation. Rather than dominating and taking whatever we want for our selfish ways, we can begin to ponder our actions and their consequences for the planet, both now and for those to come. God's transformative power instills in us the will to change. As role models in pursuing positive alterations, we should motivate others to change. God's Spirit is the source of life and a source of new life within all of us. We feel God's presence through God's Spirit as much as through God's wisdom.

Holy Spirit as Light

Light in the Scripture is associated with the Spirit of God and understood to be the divine light. The Spirit came down upon the people as tongues of fire or as light and gave birth to the church. The light as Spirit was powerful and moved people; it gave them the energy, direction, vision, and pathway to make a difference in the world. The Spirit as light is still powerful and moves people to do the work of the Spirit in this world.

Light has the capacity to both foster life and destroy life. I grew up in Sunday school singing the song, "This Little Light of Mine." I taught it to my children and to all the children I cared for in Sunday school. Some traditions, such as that of the Religious Society of Friends (Quakers), associate the Holy Spirit with light. The Quakers talk about the light of Christ and use light as an allegory to better describe the workings of the Holy Spirit.

The Holy Spirit functions as light to illuminate, particularly in relation to Scripture. The Holy Spirit both inspired the writing of the Scriptures and works to lead people into the truth of Christ as we read the holy texts. The light opens the Scriptures so that we may read in the Spirit in which they were written (2 Pet 1:20–21).

The light is a concentrated source of power and fulfillment, which reveals sin, evil, and the way to salvation. Though darkness is a formidable opponent, light continues to conquer it even in our everyday lives, filling us with God's goodness and salvation.

Being in the light, which comes from Christ, is a state of being whereby a person will come to delight in God and the power that comes of God. To find true peace is to be in the light and receive that power. The light offers God's comfort to the soul, which no mortal can equally support. The light can lead us out of the darkness into salvation and teach us to worship in Spirit and in Truth (John 4:24).

Acts 2 recounts the early church's experience of the presence and power of the Holy Spirit after the resurrection of Jesus. The Pentecost event reveals that the experience of the Spirit of God is not only personal; it is also an experience for the community of faith. Jesus promises in Scripture that upon his death he will send another Counselor (Comforter, *Paraclete*, or Advocate) in his place, namely the Holy Spirit (John 14:25–26). The Holy Spirit is a living experience of the Godhead.

Spirit as light is present in all of creation and has been ever present during the creation of this world. The light of the Spirit warms us and comforts us in times of trouble. It helps us recognize the urgency of the social ills present in our society by opening our eyes, encouraging us to focus our attention on the present injustices, and allowing us to see our missteps and the problems of our destructive lifestyles. The Spirit as light helps us recognize what needs to be done in the world and provides us agency to do so for the sake of God's reign.

Spirit as Light

Light of Intimacy

The light is present as intimacy between individuals, like a warm fire lighting a conversation with a friend. The light is meant to be shared with others. The warmth of intimacy is like a fire kindled and shared. Intimacy is crucial as we strive for greater community, peace, and oneness.

One of the strongest natural human desires is that of connection, and it is because of this desire that we have thrived and persisted as a race. However, as we become less dependent on communal connection for survival, we find ourselves yearning for something more, something deeper—true, meaningful closeness.

We desire intimacy because it is what keeps us alive emotionally, through connecting us to family, friends, and our community. We long to be close to each other and to share a bond. Koreans talk about this type of intimacy and connectedness as *jeong*,[5] a concept that captures the love for others as well as the enduring and endearing connection we can have for others.

Jeong is understood as a kind of "sticky" love, which is capable of holding people together in an intimate relationship. It is a phenomenal aspect of a person's experience in Korean culture. Though this is not an experience limited to Koreans, it is an experience that has been acutely embedded in Korean culture. The concept of *jeong* helps explain the relational experiences of individuals and communities in Korea. *Jeong* assists in preserving relationships and endeavoring to keep society ordered in a cohesive manner. For instance, though you might be in a bitter conflict with your friend or family member, it is *jeong* that keeps the relationship going and enduring even in such moments of dispute. It is so powerful that even though one may feel compelled to cut ties and never speak to a person again, *jeong* will bring them back together. *Jeong* is the light of intimacy within and among people that incessantly draws them back together.

When I was having bitter personal problems with a close friend, all I wanted was to end the relationship. My mind was burdened with the emotional weight of fresh hostility, prompting me to dwell on the decision to never see or speak to her again. Over this time, I went back and forth on the matter, deliberating what it would mean for both of us if we did not exist in each other's lives. But it was the *jeong* that drew us back together, even in the coldness of rash arguments and turmoil. This experience of

---

5. Chung and Cho, "Significance of *Jeong*."

jeong continues to stay with me and defines how I view and live out all of my relationships.

This bond is constructive in keeping people together even when they believe that they do not want to be connected. However, *jeong* eventually emanates and engenders an irresistible impulsion to keep relations with one another. People may acquire or build up *jeong* because of familial, social, school-related, or work-related relationships. This *jeong* can last a lifetime due to the strength of human connection and individual contexts based on love.

In many instances, *jeong* keeps relationships intact even if difficulties arise. Koreans will say, "I only stay in this relationship because of *jeong*," or "Because of *jeong*, I am still here," or, "We are in love because of *jeong*."

This is not the way that we tend to love in North America. In an individualistic society, *jeong* is absent; whereas in a communal society, among Koreans, *jeong* is ever present. Perhaps the West can nurture this type of love healthily, strengthening relationships that are unstable or lack the attention to continue, including communities that we have grown apart from. We all could cultivate this kind of love, a love that elicits intimate relationships and mutual compassion. If we take the other, our neighbors, and the idea of community seriously, we can begin to cultivate this kind of love. In putting this concept into practice, we can cultivate *jeong* and recognize its bonding actions in our communities, families, and other relationships.

In Korea, *woo-ri* is the nation's understanding of community over individuality. Things are addressed as being a part of community. In the West, there seems to be a tendency to say, "my church, my home, my sister, etc." In contrast, in Korea, we say, "*our* church, *our* home, *our* sister, etc." even if we are talking from a singular pronoun possessive perspective. Even though we may be the only child, we still say, "our father" rather than "my father." Even though we alone may be married to one husband, we say, "our husband" rather than, "my husband." The Korean cultural consciousness affirms that we live in community and in relation to one another. In a communal culture, we all belong to each other.

We need this love so that we can build solidarity. We long to connect with one another intimately and spiritually. The light within us can help achieve this level of intimacy. The light of the Spirit attracts us to one another and keeps us connected and interconnected. The light keeps us together and maintains the bonds between relationships even when they seem to be at their weakest.

Spirit as Light

Light and the Quakers

The general conception of divine light is not new; it was found in Plato, the neo-Platonists, St. Augustine, and many others.[6] George Fox and the early Quakers talked about light's significance in their spirituality. They associated light with Christ and believed they needed to rely on "the inner light of Christ" and the spontaneous movement of the Holy Spirit to inspire people to "minister" (i.e., pray or speak) in Quaker meetings for worship. They wanted to return to early Christianity, before the churches got organized and became more like an organization. William Penn stated in 1694:

> The Light of Christ within, who is the Light of the world and so a light to you that tells you the truth of your condition, leads all that take heed unto it out of darkness into God's marvelous light, for light grows upon the obedient.[7]

Penn associated the light with Christ and believed the light would lead us into the right path. The light shines into people's vision, and they are illumined by the Lord.[8] The light that the world yearns after is already shining. It is shining into the darkness, but the darkness does not comprehend it. The light is shining in many souls and stirring many people to become new. It is shining in many small groups and creating a fellowship of children of the light. The light will direct people to serve those in need.[9]

The concept of the inner or "inward" Light has been fundamental to Quaker spirituality. It is still there in the Advices and Queries (which is the nearest thing the Quakers have to a creed, though it is rather an expression of a whole way of life).[10] Fox emphasized that the light he was talking about is the divine Light, not natural, and that it can be described as the Light of Christ. It is sometimes called the "inner" or the "inward" light—the latter more accurately expressing the claim to its origin from outside the mind and hence its objectivity, truth, or validity.[11]

---

6. Stevenson, *Open to New Light*, 118.
7. Britain Yearly Meeting, "Reflections" 26.44.
8. Britain Yearly Meeting, "Reflections" 26.48.
9. Britain Yearly Meeting, "Reflections" 26.48.
10. Stevenson, *Open to New*, 118.
11. Stevenson, *Open to New*, 120.

Reimagining Spirit

Light vs. Dark

With the spiritual point of view, when we see physical light, we can be reminded of the presence (Spirit) of God. We live in a culture permeated with dualism. We think in dualistic ways, such as "man is good and woman is evil"; "the word is rational and is therefore good, whereas wisdom is emotion and therefore not desirable"; or "light is good and darkness is evil." In such a binary-filled world, the image of light as Spirit can also become problematic.

Light as good and darkness as evil is an over-simplified worldview. This duality is used often in contemporary culture to bolster one and undermine the other. One eminent example is the movie, *Star Wars IV: A New Beginning* (and virtually all the movies in the Star Wars saga, especially *Star Wars VII*). In *A New Beginning*, Darth Vader, the clear villain, is dressed in black from head to toe. This explicit imagery doesn't just allude to the simplest notion that black is equated with evil and badness or parallels to Adolf Hitler's totalitarian reign but also has cultural and racial connotations. It has been discussed as a problematic visual element of this celebrated series, expressing that it is the people of color who fight against white privilege, white supremacy, and systemic racism.

The world, with its very short attention span, seems to downplay the marginal voices. People of color are oppressed and made to live in the peripheries of society while the dominant, white society continues to enjoy their privilege without discerning its significance or consequence. White privilege uses its authority to limit the accessibility and mobility of the marginalized to move upwards socially and economically. Unchallenged white privilege can lead to atrocities such as literal and economic slavery—especially that of women. It has been used to hold others under their power, sustain control, and maintain the status quo.

Using skin color to determine status in society is an intolerable way of maintaining power over others. Transculturally, fair skin is the preference. In most of Asia, light skin is associated with the aristocratic class and dark skin with agricultural workers and the lower class. This visual connotation has historically influenced the beauty ideals in nearly all of Asia, which idolizes fair skin and patronizes those with tanned or darker skin.

In ancient Rome, olive-colored skin, such as that of Padma Lakshmi,[12] was considered ideal, while the whiter skin of folk from the north was

---

12. Padma Lakshmi is an American author, actress, and model of Indian descent.

considered inferior. How can we view each other without considering the color of skin? Rating and ranking status according to skin color is unfair, discriminatory, and problematic. We have to level the playing field. It is time our education systems, Sunday schools, and workforces teach us how to live with and affirm the value of each person so that we can become stronger citizens of the world. In order to do this, we need to learn to love each other and welcome each other as equals.

The light, which is the Spirit of God, shows us how we need to embrace all people, no matter the color of our skin. We seek goodness in everyone and in everything. We work with all so that we are able to stand together in solidarity. By allowing the Spirit to work with us and use us, we can do the work of justice, mercy, and good will. Light gives us life, healing, and replenishment.

Light of Justice

How we think about the Holy Spirit is an important part of Christian theology. When Christians speak of God as Spirit, we do not speak of "one third" of God but of the full presence of God. To speak of God as Spirit conveys the power and mystery of God's universal, active, and relational presence. The Spirit language is not about a vague or hidden God; rather, it intimately communicates that God's presence within us is the Light.

As we explore the divine, we come to understand that it is vast in its complex, ambiguous, and incomprehensible existence. If this is so, why would there be a belief in an orthodox way of talking about the divine? In a multidimensional world, how is it possible that Christians possess the only way to come to understand God? Can we understand that the Spirit is present in all cultures and religions? Is it possible? Doesn't this imply that the Spirit is the basis for converging thoughts about the divine? Perhaps we can talk in partnership with other religions on a journey to a deeper understanding of the divine.

Our lives are conditioned by our experiences. This includes communities of people as well as all of God's creation. The attempt to dominate creation as if we have no connection to its fate is foolhardy. The clearer we understand symbiosis, the better off we will be. Many of our planetary problems arise because of the denial of our interdependence with all creation, and we continue to perceive it as an object of domination. This simple worldview of Earth as an exploitable resource is a manifestation of our own shortsightedness and greed, setting the precedent in our line of thinking. It is this dangerous line of thinking that got us to the volatile environment we are in.

The sooner we recognize this interdependence with creation, the quicker we can work toward preserving this planet and ourselves. We cannot exist in a vacuum. If we are going to decolonize our minds, we need to work together to rid ourselves of an individualistic mindset and move toward a communal understanding of interdependence. By doing so, we can build healthier, friendlier, and kinder ways of living.

We tend to separate the spirit world and the world of matter. We believe that these matters operate distinctly, without overlap. But as we begin to critique dualism and its resulting consequences within our own theologies, we invite global perspectives into the conversation. As we examine other views, we recognize that there need not be a distinct separation between the spirit world and the world of matter. The purpose and wisdom used in dealing with the natural world is identical to what we employ when assessing matters of the Spirit. The body and mind are integrated, being two sides of the same coin. This view brings a new perspective and depth to the incarnation and our understanding of the Holy Spirit.

The light that lives in each of us moves us to bring forth new life. Both our own moral intuition and the light of the Spirit will guide us in the ways we work for justice. Quaker theologian George Fox used the phrase "that of God" in everyone. "That of God" may be interpreted as the spark of human spirituality, the Spirit, and the Light that exists in all people. Though we are not fully sure of how it has come to exist, we are secure in knowing that the divine is present and exists in all of us.

As we recognize the divine in all of us, we recognize the other as part of ourselves. As we understand and grasp this concept for our lives, it will transform us to work towards positive objectives. We are to love one another and be in solidarity with one another, especially with the poor. At times, it is difficult to do the work of justice. At such times, it is the light of the Holy Spirit within us that gives us the power to work for justice. It is not an easy road, but it is a road that will help build the reign of God here on Earth.

To become one with the light and be in communion with the Divine, we need to live in the light. To live in the light is to do what God asks of us. That is to love God with our whole heart, soul, and mind, loving our neighbors as ourselves. We work to dismantle the hierarchies that exist in all facets of life—those hierarchies that separate men and women, dominancy and minority, straight and LGBTQ+, humanity and creation. We move towards inclusion and equality. We move towards equilibrium.

The light will help us achieve this equilibrium, as the wisdom it provides will help us achieve greater justice. God will help us to move toward the goodness that exists. Building the reign of God will move us towards goodness and faithfulness. Building the reign of God can be done as we follow God's commandments and the Sermon on the Mount (Matt 5:3–10). We need to become poor in spirit, be merciful, hunger for righteousness, and stride confidently as peacemakers. Ask the Holy Spirit to show you how to embrace those who are different. Learn from them and see how enriched this life is. It is a better life, and it is a cause of celebration.

The Holy Spirit as light is a mighty and formidable concept. Listening for and following the guidance of the Holy Spirit will help us achieve goodness and mercy in our world. Moving towards reconciliation, justice, and bridge-building, we become the best possible versions of ourselves, and in moving towards the light of God, we will become empowered to do God's work.

The Holy Spirit is also a prophetic voice that can empower the ministry of the followers of Jesus. It inspires the community, weak as we may appear to be, to do the work of God: to feed the poor, clothe the naked, and care for the sick. It empowers us to be intimate with each other and to be in solidarity with those whom society has pushed to the margins. It allows us to move towards goodness and to join God in bringing the story of goodness to life and acknowledging it in our world. The presence of God as the light empowers us to move towards social justice and work for God's love. It assures us that the God of love, the Spirit of love, will always guide us to hope, sustenance, and love. The love of the Spirit of God will keep us trusting God. It will help us have faith in God and live together joyfully as we follow Jesus in community.

The Spirit, as the light, strengthens us as we work for justice. The world and its inhabitants, as imperfect as they are, can look to the Spirit to strengthen the fight against systemic injustice. When we depend on the light for our strength, we are walking with God. The Spirit is light, and it provides us guidance and carves a counseled path where we are to walk with God. The light brightens our walk with God. It nourishes us so that we can walk with God and move forward. Spirit as light is a reimagining of our understanding of the Holy Spirit. The light is before us and behind us.

Reimagining Spirit

It will guide us every day, every waking moment. The Holy Spirit as light will provide spiritual nourishment as it gives life. Light is the source and provider of life, bestowing the goodness and love that will empower us to move towards greater justice and equity.

Racial Injustice

The Holy Spirit as light sheds light on the racial injustices that occur in this world, where whiteness is preferred and those who are of a different color are tyrannized and subjugated. There is a deeply embedded fear and oppression of people with dark skin. In America, there have been countless attacks on unarmed, young black men and women. At times, it feels nearly impossible to keep up with the news of police shootings or abuses of authority affecting the black community—and we should know that the mainstream media only shares a small fraction of it.

Stephon Clark was with his grandparents and siblings in his own backyard when the Sacramento police fatally shot him, mistaking a cell phone for a weapon. The police were responding to a report that someone was breaking car windows nearby.[13] How could this possibly happen to someone who was on his own property? Someone who felt safe in his own home, surrounded by his family? Yet again, this event peeled back the curtain of the racial prejudice and lack of competent education that exists in our justice system, and it is the marginalized minority that have to pay the price.

Diante Yarber is another tragic example of an unarmed black man shot to death by the police. Yarber hit a police car while accelerating in reverse.[14] The Barstow Police fired on his vehicle, which contained three unarmed passengers, more than two dozen times. Even if Yarber did drive towards the officers, it did not warrant the multiplicity of shots fired, and it certainly did not warrant his death.

While the hideous history of Black Americans being terrorized in America sadly prevails today, the history of colonialism and the genocide of Native Americans are seldom discussed in popular discourse. There has been mass murder, abuse, and rape of Native Americans from the beginning of conquest in the Americas.

13. Cerullo, "Unarmed Black Man."
14. "Family of Unarmed Black Man."

Spirit as Light

This horrible devastation is difficult to fathom for most, as time and neglectful teachings of this part of history has muffled Native Americans as a people. Digging back to the meaning of "redskins," we should be privy to its significance: the murder of a Native American for bounty. Scalping had been a known practice in Europe, and the white conquerors in America offered to pay "bounties" for Native Americans.[15] In order to get paid, white conquerors had to show that they had actually killed an Indian. They first brought their bodies, but when their bodies were too heavy to carry, they brought just their heads. When the heads got too heavy to carry, they began scalping the Indians and bringing the "red skins" to prove they had killed an Indian so they would be paid their bounty.

White Americans further humiliated the surviving Native Americans by violently forcing them to leave their families and communities and sending their children to boarding schools, where they would be horribly abused and assimilated into American culture, erasing everything they knew about their own. Randy S. Woodley writes, "For almost 100 years, in the name of progress, Native children were forced into government-sponsored, denominationally-run boarding schools, where many were abused physically, sexually, emotionally, and spiritually, and where many of them died. The rallying cry to civilize/Christianize Indigenous children was 'kill the Indian, save the child.'"[16]

Racism, colonialism, and patriarchy intersect. Sexual violence, for one, is not simply a tool of patriarchy but also a tool of colonialism and racism. This means that all communities of color are the victims of sexual violence. A perpetuated falsehood leads to the fabrication: raping dirty bodies is "acceptable" because such bodies do not count and they are not entitled to bodily integrity.[17] The rape of Native American women to control and assert power over them to continuously subordinate them is abominable. The consequences of these actions have left a dark stain on American history, a tragic pain that has been perpetually left untreated and that is still felt intensely today.

Many Native Americans have not just been forgotten in history but also have been dismantled and reduced as a population. This, in the minds of the colonialist, justifies the conquest of native lands. Natives are often portrayed as sexual deviants—blamed for their sexual sins—dirty, lazy,

---

15. Martin, "Scalping," 189.
16. Woodley, "Native American Christianity."
17. Smith, *Conquest*, 8–10.

substance/alcohol abusing, uncivilized, and stupid.[18] The negative portrayal of Native Americans legitimizes the dominant white culture's attitude and actions towards them. These various forms of racism are dangerous, as they perpetuate stereotypes and allow for the continued subordination of Native Americans to whites. The sins of racism are revealed to us through the light of the Spirit, who continues to show us how we function and take missteps in living the right way.

We need to fight against colonialism, for it devalues cultures, persons, and histories. It not only disempowers people but also subjugates and exploits them. Communities and lives have been broken. We need to work toward wholeness and healing for the peoples who have been systematically abused.

We must love those who are so different from us.

We should embrace and care for the foreigner.

We must love the wounded and those who are so devastated and broken.

We need to gain back the righteousness that was lost. We must help those who are stranded. We need to love them and welcome them into our land. We have to understand that some are fighting for their lives. We must embrace those who are so different from us and fight the racism that has destroyed us.

Sexual Injustice

With the #MeToo movement, countless women and men who have been kept silent for years are finally emerging with their stories, making the world aware of the rampant sexual abuse of those in power. We need to fight for gender equality and ensure that we make it safe for all women on this planet to live with no hesitation, freely, and without fear.

Perhaps there is no example of sexual abuse by those in power more infamous than the case that ignited the movement—that of Bill Cosby. I grew up with *The Cosby Show*. Bill Cosby was a powerful, iconic cultural influence for my generation. I used to sit in front of the TV and laugh along with the laugh track, mindlessly thinking to myself, "Wow, he would be such a cool dad." He had an uncanny smile, a contagious chuckle, and always shot back with the perfect response.

---

18. Smith, *Conquest*, 9.

Of course, the notoriety of Bill Cosby and his malicious past is not an isolated case. A great number of men and women with power, stature, and wealth have been convicted of or accused of committing illegal sexual acts towards young, vulnerable women and men. While the world fell into shock as their idolized figures had their veiled pasts revealed, it is vital that as allegations continue to surface, we take them seriously and have them investigated and brought to court if the alleged actions are unlawful.[19] We have heard the allegations against Woody Allen, Roman Polanski, Penn State University football coach Jerry Sandusky, and the list goes on.

We can only discourage similar acts by others if celebrity does not shield against criminal prosecution. As a society, we follow and accept celebrities or other people who are granted such titles as "role models." As we get to know them, we need to recognize that many have "feet of clay"—in other words, they have major character flaws. Therefore, there will be an evident disconnect between one's past experiences of Cosby as a TV dad and the implications of these allegations, radically shifting how we relate to perceived or actual role models. As we recognize that some of our most revered figures have systematically abused their power to keep their dark histories private, we need to work at revolutionizing a system that protects the affluent and give voice to those who seek justice.

As a mom of a young girl who loves to dance and perform, I am constantly aware of men who may take advantage of her desire to entertain and please an audience. Young girls like my daughter are eager to succeed and put trust in those with authority, power, and prestige. They may, without knowing, fall into the trap of giving in—giving in to what someone in authority might ask for, what they desire, what they promise is "best" for them.

This is the vulnerability of young girls who fall victim to men of power. Religion has a long history of justifying the submission of women, which has led to a culture of sexual oppression, particularly that of women and children. We need to continuously address this long patriarchal aspect within Christianity and work towards dismantling it. We must fight to address such subordination of women and eliminate protection of the affluent within our society, culture, and religion.

In our society, which continues to shame or blame the victim—as Don Lemon on CNN did in his interview with Joan Tarshis[20]—it is crucial to

---

19. A version of this text first appeared in Kim, "Uncovering Bill Cosby's Feet of Clay."
20. Fowler and Egan, "CNN's Don Lemon Apologizes."

teach our sons and daughters their value as human beings. We need to ask ourselves how much longer we can tolerate a social system that normalizes and protects abusers of power. We cannot continue to allow women to be seen as mere sexual objects to be used by men for their pleasure and then dismissed—or paid off—when they are abused, raped, or pushed to report their abuse.

As mothers, fathers, daughters, sons, and human beings, we need to challenge the systematic exploitation of power that allows felonious acts to be suppressed by hidden settlements or unjudged by a public court of law. Such underpinnings need to be dismantled and restructured. We need to move away from a culture with disparate categorical standards and move towards an egalitarian society. We need to teach all people that sexual activity must be fully consensual. We need to develop a culture in which we take seriously those who make allegations of rape and sexual violation. We need to support those who come forward and to ensure that their allegations are fully, fairly, and transparently investigated. When appropriate, adjudication and punishment should follow.

Power, privilege, and prestige provide no exception to how we treat one another. They should not provide protection when allegations of violations are made. Each of us is entitled to safety, respect, and dignity. We are all God's children. The Spirit as light enlightens us to the tragedies of inequity that exist throughout the world, for those who have been disregarded, trivialized, and silenced.

Climate Change

One of the most crucial issues of our time is climate change. Climate change can be defined as long-term weather patterns that have been changed for an extended period (usually 10 years or longer). These patterns can have dangerous affects in one region, surrounding regions, or the entire Earth.

Climate change is caused by changes in the amount of energy kept within the Earth's atmosphere. As humans create more carbon dioxide (CO_2) and other greenhouse gases, we continue to contribute to the worsening climate on Earth. We see an assured danger to all of creation as the climate continues to change.

Atmospheric CO_2 functions much like the glass of a greenhouse. It allows the sun's heat to come in but prevents much of it from radiating back out to space. We need atmospheric CO_2, for without it, the Earth would be

Spirit as Light

an ice-cold, lifeless rock. However, over the past 150 years, the sky has had too much CO_2 and the Earth has been overheating.[21]

The Pew Center on Global Climate Change states, "The Earth's average surface temperature has increased by 1.4 degrees Fahrenheit (0.8 degree Celsius) since the early years of the twentieth century. The eleven warmest years on record since (1850) have all occurred in the past thirteen years. The five warmest years to date are 2005, 1998, 2002, 2003, 2007."[22] This rapid increase in temperature will have devastating effects on Earth's biosphere.

For some, less than 1 Celsius degree warmer over a hundred-year period may not sound devastating, but scientists believe that it is exactly enough to initiate the disruption of the climate system's equilibrium. Greenland and Antarctic ice sheets are important for reflecting large amounts of solar radiation back into space and regulating the flow of ocean currents, yet with warming temperatures, they are melting at rates much faster than climate scientists had predicted.

This loss of reflective ice means that more solar radiation is becoming absorbed, which means that the world will continue to heat faster. Polar ice is melting rapidly, disgorging billions of gallons of fresh water, altering the chemistry and currents of the oceans, adding volume and threatening to raise sea levels by up to a meter over this century. Climate change is affecting us through its extreme weather swings, ocean acidification, melting glaciers, and rising sea levels. Disruptive climate change is certain—even if we make the economic shift away from fossil fuels.[23]

Earth's climate will have an enormous impact on the poor, limiting the choices that will enable them to rise above the poverty line. Along with the ramifications of climate change on the underprivileged, there is also the problem of deforestation. The market drives the need to convert native forests into agricultural lands without taking into consideration the need to maintain forests for the environment.[24]

For the first half of the twenty-first century, it is not likely that climate change will affect the global food supply. Reduction in low-latitude food production will likely be offset by increases in production in middle to high latitudes. However, climate change in the second half of the century could

---

21. Parenti, *Tropic of Chaos*, 5.
22. Parenti, *Tropic of Chaos*, 6.
23. Parenti, *Tropic of Chaos*, 6.
24. Brainard et al., *Climate Change and Global Poverty*, 14, 17.

start to affect global food production, especially if the warming is on the higher end of expectations. As global food supplies fall, food prices will increase, creating intense adversity for poor households.[25]

In September 2014, UN Secretary-General Ban Ki-moon held a climate summit with prominent world leaders in New York City. The work of international leaders must continue beyond a climate summit with deep dedication and commitment to lower greenhouse gases and pursue sustainability and environmental justice. Those who are in positions of power must push to develop an international plan to account for "out of state" pollution that crosses borders to befoul air and water. The current lack of agency to make changes and plan proactively will result in the complete devastation of our planet and the life that inhabits it.

Without the commitment and work of each nation, each government, each community, and every individual, we will move quickly down the road to environmental collapse. The concept of climate justice does not just relate to the changes in climate but also to the industrial and commercial activities of highly industrialized nations environmentally impacting other countries that have done nothing to create those effects. Climate change has a hold over humanity's wellness, displaces the state of the ecosystem, and destroys the Earth's natural resources. Climate change affects human rights such as food, water, and sanitation, as well as the right to a safe environment. Climate change is a clear example of the extraterritorial effects of our actions against the environment. Climate justice assumes that laws rarely bridge[26] national borders, yet countries should still be held accountable for damaging the health and welfare of other countries.

In 1992, at the Rio Summit, the United Nations' Framework Convention on Climate Change emerged to tackle the issue of reducing greenhouse gas concentrations in the atmosphere. The Conference of the Parties (COP) was designated as the supreme governing body of the Convention. This initiative has led to some positive results. In 1997, the Kyoto Protocol, a binding instrument of the Convention, was adopted. The Protocol established how much industrialized countries should reduce their CO_2 emissions.

At COP, delegates from 195 countries meet annually to share information on greenhouse gas emissions, national policies, and optimal practices, as well as to negotiate how to prevent further damage to ecological

---

25. Mendelsohn, "Development in the Balance," 121.

26. International affairs on the environment are under international organizations and international treaties.

systems to protect agriculture from climate change. Discussions focus on adaptation, mitigation, climate finance, and technology transfer to support developing countries to combat practices that compound climate change's advancement.

We live in a time when a certain level of convenience and comfort are expected and control a long line of many small life choices. Wherever we are living, most of us want to live in a comfortable room temperature of around 68 degrees Fahrenheit (20 degrees Celsius). Consequently, we use the Earth's resources to make sure we live and sleep within this narrow comfort zone with little regard to what it does to our Earth and the effects it has on our climate. Adapting a lifestyle that lowers dependency on burned fuel (fossil or wood) and all other types of open air burning is a basic step that nations and individuals can take to live a more ecologically conscious life.

As we seek to identify other steps, we need to recognize that technology can be one of our greatest assets, offering us ever-progressing methods for energy conservation and renewable energy.

As we live on this Earth, it is the Spirit as light that reveals to us the explicit present danger we cause with our lifestyle. When we let in the light of the Spirit and make an honest assessment of our complicity in climate change, we will see our position as perpetrators of our present ecological crisis.

The understanding of God as the Spirit may help us work toward a better eco-theology which will sustain all of us living on this Earth. Psalm 104:29–30 says, "When you take away their breath, they die and return to dust. When you send forth your breath, they are created and you renew the face of the earth."

Light and the Reign of God

We all participate in building the reign of God on Earth, and it is the Spirit that helps us build this rule. We experience the Spirit just as we experience love, joy, peace, patience, kindness, goodness, and faithfulness. The wisdom of God exhibits these characteristics. A prophetic ministry is inspired by the leading of the Holy Spirit. The authority for ministry comes from Christ, the Logos, through the Holy Spirit. It places in us the same Spirit the apostles had. The Spirit helps us to move and engage in the ministry of Christ.

John 1:4 says, "In him was life, and the life was the light of all people." "Wherever his spirit appears, the oppressed gather fresh courage; for he announced that fear, hypocrisy, and hatred, the three hounds of hell that track the trail of the disinherited, need have no dominion over them."[27] When we as Christians choose to highlight the aspect of Christ as light or as Word made flesh, we can, with Howard Thurman, join in proclaiming and witnessing the authentic life-giving and liberating qualities of the gospel message we find in John's Gospel and elsewhere.

In John 8:12, Jesus says, "I am the light of the world. Whoever follows me will never walk in darkness but will have the light of life." 1 John 1:7 talks about how we should "walk in the light." The inner light of God within will lead us to become disciples who are empowered to do the work of justice. Wisdom and the Logos alone may reveal the right way, but we need to allow the light to draw us forward so we can march together against injustice and help build and sustain the reign of God. The Holy Spirit as light illumines the problems that we face on Earth, such as the problems of social injustice, climate injustice, and gender injustice.

Conclusion

Spirit as light is in all of creation and has been forever present even before the creation of this world. It is the light of the Spirit that helps us recognize the urgency of climate change. The Spirit illuminates our minds and hearts, allowing us to see our missteps and the problems of our destructive lifestyles. It helps us recognize what needs to be done in the world for the sake of God's reign. Images of enlightenment and illumination will guide us in better understanding that the Spirit as light is powerful.

Like a sacrament in the broadest sense, the physical points beyond itself to the spiritual. In our case, the light points to the Spirit. As the light enables us to see physically, we will be acquainted spiritually through God's light. We see the Spirit of God at work. The Spirit enlightens in the New Testament. The Spirit points to Jesus Christ; therefore, the Spirit witnesses to Christ. Christ is God.

The Spirit enlightens by giving faith and new life in Christ. This gives our lives new direction (the "new creation" of Scripture), salvation—everything associated with newness of life. This is all achieved by the work of the Spirit, who brings light to our darkness.

27. Thurman, *Jesus and the Disinherited*, 28.

Spirit as Light

We are to "live as children of light" (Eph 5:8)—that is, walk in the Spirit and live in the presence of God. This is only possible because the Spirit lives in us: "Do you not know that you are God's temple and that God's Spirit dwells in you?" (1 Cor 3:16), as it is the inner light.

The Spirit as light embraces the whole world, giving us hope for a better tomorrow. The Spirit works to engender peace, justice, love, and reason. The inner life is God's Spirit at work, and the light reminds us of physical light, which we should see as a pointed indicator (through sacrament) towards God's wide Spirit, engaging us, society, the church, and the world.

Light is a wonderful and familiar image to help us connect. Scripturally, the Spirit is a witness to Jesus Christ. Spirit as light shows us the truth. Light renders the ability to see—even to see where the Spirit is active in the world. Thus, reciprocity is present. The Spirit brings light to the mind and heart, and the physical light enables us to see the Spirit at work around us. As we become cognizant of the Spirit's work in each other and in the world, we can come to love one another the way Scripture entreats us.

The creation of human beings began with the breath of God exhaled into us. The breath kept us alive and continues to sustain us. It keeps us motioning forward and provides the goodness within us. It urges us to share it with the rest of the world, to create a better future, and to build better lives for our next generations. The Spirit as light is the Spirit of God within us. It sheds light on us and provides the goodness of God's mercy upon us. It is the Light that moves us to work in the world, to look past ourselves, and to work for sustainability, nurture, and love for all.

CHAPTER 3

Spirit as Wind and Breath

Holy Spirit as Wind

OUR CHRISTIAN UNDERSTANDING OF the Holy Spirit comes from the Old and New Testaments of the Bible, the life of the church, and our experiences of that Spirit. The Bible helps us understand the Holy Spirit and how she works.

When I was a young girl, my experience of the Holy Spirit was marked by the binary differences between the "fun" and the "scary" church. My parents brought me and my sister along to their Pentecostal revival services, where I first saw the jarring physical reactions to the spoken word. I remember feeling the crushing terror as I peeked into the private room of adults, speaking in tongues with their hands raised in the air, shaking and collapsing to the floor. Then I remember seeing my parents in the room, the back of their familiar heads, trembling involuntarily. Seeing this, I was convinced that there was something sinister about church, something that was taking a hold of my mom and dad, urging me to get out and leave. However, as a young child, fleeing the church was clearly not an option. So I stayed with my parents and experienced years of occasional Pentecostal revival services. While my introduction to the Holy Spirit was shrouded in fear and uncertainty, my current understanding has matured far past the place it began in. I later saw experiences that were profoundly powerful but did not involve such bodily manifestations. It challenged my preconceptions about its formidable influence, giving to me peace and newfound clarity, which I eventually saw being brought into other people's lives. What does the Bible say about the Holy Spirit?

The Scriptures depict an image of what the Spirit is and what the Spirit does. The Spirit is ever-present and moves within creation. It is through these earliest connections with nature and the natural world that the Hebrew people experienced God. We who live in modern and developed geographies have lost touch with what is becoming increasingly rarified: the natural world. As we become more digital creatures and rely on increasingly more convenient technology, the time we spend connecting to nature and spending time outside is vastly reduced. We are becoming estranged to the natural space we inhabit, losing touch with how enormously we depend on it, and ultimately how much we are damaging it. We often forget as well that within nature, there is God in the plants, animals, and complex ecosystems with whom we share the world. We have even forgotten that creation exists because of God.

An understanding of the Holy Spirit as wind can bring us back to a primordial, earthy reality. We can be in touch with nature again and realize that the Holy Spirit as wind is found in everything and is everywhere. The association of *ruach* as the Holy Spirit in the imagery of wind continues in the New Testament with the Greek word *pneuma*. The Spirit blows where it wills (John 3:8), and at Pentecost, the Spirit comes like a wind (Acts 2:2). This chapter will examine this understanding of the Spirit as wind as found in Scripture and as witnessed in the church's experiences.

Wind and the Exodus Story

The Holy Spirit appears often throughout the Bible. It occurs 380 times in the Hebrew Bible as the Hebrew word *ruach*, which is translated as "breath," "wind," "soul," or "spirit," to speak of the Holy Spirit. *Ruach* probably derived from an onomatopoetic sound of a gale, like the strong wind that divided the Red Sea during the exodus from Egypt (Exod 14:21).[1]

The tribe of Israel (Jacob) moved to Egypt during a time of famine, as told in the story of Joseph and his brothers at the end of Genesis. After spending many generations in Egypt, a new Pharaoh eventually enslaved the Hebrews there. As slaves, they suffered and sought out ways to freedom. At this time, God, by way of the burning bush, called Moses to deliver the Hebrew people out of Egypt (Exod 3:7–12). At first, Moses was reluctant

---

1. Moltmann, *Spirit of Life*, 40.

to obey God, but he eventually responded to God's call and mustered the courage to ask Pharaoh to let God's people go. When Pharaoh chose not to let the slaves go, God sent plagues upon the Egyptians. After the tenth horrible plague, the death of all firstborn Egyptians and all their livestock (Exod 12:29), Pharaoh finally relented.

As the Hebrews fled Egypt, they eventually came to the edge of the Red Sea. To their horror, Pharaoh had a change of heart and sent his army after them in war chariots (Exod 14:5–9). While they stood in terror at the shore of the Red Sea with the Egyptians bearing down behind them, Moses lifted his staff in the air and parted the waters:

> Then Moses stretched out his hand over the sea. The LORD drove the sea back by a strong east wind all night, and turned the sea into dry land; and the waters were divided. (Exod 14:21)

It was the strong wind that made a clear pathway and escape for the fleeing Hebrew people. Their word *ruach* imitated the "whoosh" or blowing sound made by a forceful wind. This force can be viewed as the power of the almighty God.

Wind appears in several different places throughout the Old Testament (e.g., Gen 8:1; Num 11:31; Isa 27:8). This dual meaning of the word *ruach* is evident, for example, in Exodus 15: "At a breath [*ruach*] of your anger the waters piled up. . . . When your wind [ruach] blew, the sea covered them" (Exod 15:8, 10).[2]

The Hebrew people stood in amazement at the power of the wind that provided a way toward freedom. The wind was a loud, awe-full sound that reminded the people that God was around them all the time. The wind blows every day. It blows all around us whether or not we can actually hear it or see its effects. All creation experiences God's presence as it hovers over the Earth and moves as it wills.

This image of the Holy Spirit as redemptive power is best seen in this account of the exodus. You can see the actions of God through the effects that are present within all people and the world. These manifestations of the Holy Spirit were practical and useful for the Hebrew people. They affirmed that God is present, would not abandon them, and would continue to work in their lives. However, as much as they recognized God in the currents of wind, they also experienced difficulties with the wind. After their escape,

---

2. Karkkainen, *Pneumatology*, 14.

they spent forty years wandering in the wilderness, where they were both dominated and liberated by the power of the wind.

BorderLinks Desert Walk

If you have ever walked in a desert, you will know that the wind and sand are a ubiquitous source of potential danger. There are deserts that are mostly rolling, shifting sand dunes, such as the Sahara Desert, the largest subtropical hot desert. The Sahara has long stretches of sand and dunes dotted with irregular, widely-placed oases. However, there are also rocky, stony deserts with cacti and other thorny succulents that can survive in the dry heat.

Perhaps the most dangerous marriage of the desert and the wind is the sandstorm. Sand looks and feels harmless under foot, but in a desert wind, the storm picks up sand particles and dust as fine as talcum powder. This inescapable whirl of sand and fine grit and dust finds its way into the eyes, nose, mouth, and even into the inner workings of any machinery, such as automobiles, cameras, or bicycles.

A few years ago, I took several seminary and college students to Nogales, Mexico, with the BorderLinks[3] Program to study immigration and the plight of Central Americans as they crossed the desert into the United States. BorderLinks took us on a short walk in the desert for a firsthand experience of the difficulties and hardships. Even a seemingly serene desert is filled with countless things in constant motion, active everywhere in this dry and barren setting.

The staff leaders of our excursion into the desert warned us to wear long pants, as cacti and thorny bushes cling to your legs and cause painful lacerations. Not fully acknowledging the dangers and precautions of this environment, several wore shorts, thinking that they would be safe.

Within five minutes, those wearing shorts were quickly faced with the perils of the desert. They began shouting out for help as the cactus needles attached themselves to their skin. It was an unbelievable sight. The BorderLinks staff leader helped free them from the thorny cacti, giving us all a taste of the reality, a glimpse into what it is like being present and walking in the fervent desert.

The staff leader from BorderLinks explained that when the United States Border Patrol seeks out people crossing into the United States, they hover low with helicopters, causing the sand to swirl violently, going into

3. For more information about BorderLinks, see www.borderlinks.org.

people's eyes, as if they were in the eye of a sandstorm. Cacti, loose branches, and thorns are caught up in the air, generated by the rotors. As a result, migrants panic and scatter sporadically. Some lose each other in the desert, while some do not survive at all. This tactic is used to discourage any entry into the United States. As the helicopters hover over the desert, traveling immigrants experience the destructive power of the wind.

Reading stories of the Hebrew people wandering in the desert for forty years resonates with such experiences of the wind's dominance. They recognized the power of the Spirit of God as wind, vibrating throughout all creation. Along with this acknowledgement came the fear of the Spirit of God as God manifested God's presence through the wind. Either way, they recognized that the wind was a power that blew as it wished, a force that no one human could have the ability to influence or control. Even today, with sophisticated weather forecasting models, we are still powerless in preventing the destruction that it can bring onto our environment and communities.

Holy Spirit and the Earth

Genesis portrays the Spirit as wind as it states, "The earth was a formless void and darkness covered the face of the deep, while a wind from God swept over the face of the waters" (Gen 1:2, NRSV).

The Spirit is in the breath of the wind. God created human beings and breathed life into them. "Then the LORD God formed man from the dust of the ground and breathed into his nostrils the breath of life" (Gen 2:7). The Spirit as the breath of life brings people together to act by bringing the vision of a fruitful and just life into being.

Ruach is a feminine noun employed in the first verses of Genesis to speak of the mothering, life-giving Spirit of God that hovered and brooded over the deep at creation. The Spirit as mother hovers over the Earth and gives it life. Not only does it give life, it also gives the Earth protection. Like a mother hen who protects her chicks (Ps 91:4), the Holy Spirit will act benevolently. The Spirit as wind moves through creation to give birth to new forms of life, nurturing and protecting it. This is something that we can emulate when we interact with creation. Rather than dominating creation, we need to work toward building a symbiotic relationship with it, in which we support one another and care for the well being of both partners for prosperity.

Spirit as Wind and Breath

During the Reformation, the Genevan Reformer says it is "by no means an obscure testimony which Moses bears in the history of the creation when he says that the Spirit of God was expanded over the abyss or shapeless matter."[4] Calvin speaks of the Spirit's role in creation in a way that bears a close resemblance with contemporary theologians' emphasis on the Spirit as the principle of life.[5] Calvin understood the important role that the Spirit played in all of life.

Our detachment from nature has led many of us to make the Holy Spirit into something of an intellectual or philosophical exercise. Rather than the Holy Spirit being understood as a living and participating entity, we have rendered it as an abstract idea. We have forgotten that the Holy Spirit is living, moving, and circulating all around us. Just as the Hebrew people who left Egypt witnessed the power of the Holy Spirit as the wind that parted the Red Sea, we can recognize the power of the Holy Spirit in our own daily lives.

The powerful wind blowing around us reminds us of God's presence in our lives, evoking the presence of God within all of us. The wind of the Holy Spirit comes into our bodies and gives us power, strengthening and empowering us to work for God. Allowing the Holy Spirit to move and encourage us as it intends helps us discern how to navigate our ways of living.

John 3 speaks of the enigmatic nature of wind and the Spirit's role in a believer's new birth. In this passage, John explicitly connects the image of wind with God's Spirit.[6] "The wind blows where it chooses, and you hear the sound of it, but you do not know where it comes from or where it goes. So it is with everyone who is born of the Spirit" (John 3:8). As the wind blows freely, we must recognize that while we are inclined to control all elements in our environment, we can never attain authority over the wind. We cannot direct it one way or another; it cannot be moved, as it has a mind of its own. In the same way, the Spirit as wind moves as it wishes, unable to be tamed and fully understood. Perhaps this characteristic of the Spirit is the most consequential reason it is seen as it is today, as the human desire to control and know has not been granted, making us face our own fallibility and mortality.

---

4. Calvin, *Institutes of the Christian Religion*, 122–23.

5. Karkkainen, *Pneumatology*, 72.

6. Karkkainen, *Pneumatology*, 14.

Reimagining Spirit

Spirit as Breath

Similar to the Spirit as wind is the Spirit as breath. Breathing is essential to life. It is the symbol of life—its very inauguration and its persisting existence.

During the births of my three children, the very first thing I uttered each time was, "Are they breathing?" After three long, difficult pregnancies and long, more painful deliveries, all I wanted to know was whether my baby was able to draw breath—the first indication of life. To breathe is to live by God's gift and grace.

The Spirit of God is recognized in the creation story as the breath of God—the force that gifts life to all. Without God breathing into Adam, there is no life. Thus, creation is understood as an act of God, and God is acting in the creation narrative. It is through God that everything is given life. Without God's breath there is no life. The Holy Spirit breathes and gives life abundantly to all in the cosmos and everything that exists within it (Gen 1:2).

In the Genesis 2 creation story, we find one of the earliest biblical conceptions: God breathes into the nostrils of Adam, and Adam becomes a living being (Gen 2:7). This is an extraordinary passage of how a human being comes to life through God's breathing. This passage employs the Hebrew word *neshamah*, which is translated as "breath." The initial act of God breathing life into human beings in the Genesis 2 creation story is an important prelude to John 20:22, where Jesus breathes onto the disciples and pronounces to them, "Receive the Holy Spirit." In the Old Testament, the breath of all creatures belongs to God.[7] God is the source of breath, which is life. All life comes forth from God.

God as life-giving Spirit is the proper source of life and strength; in a derivative sense, *ruach* also denotes "life force" (Num 16:22). That life force is lacking in idols (Jer 10:14), but it is in God (Ps 33:6) and in the Messiah (Isa 11:4). God is the only one who gives the life force (Isa 42:5).[8]

God creates and sustains creation through the Holy Spirit. "When you send your Spirit, they are created and you renew the face of the earth" (Ps 104:30). The life of all things and all people are in the hands of the Spirit (Job 12:10). Death comes when God withdraws God's Spirit (Job

---

7. Karkkainen, *Pneumatology*, 14.
8. Karkkainen, *Pneumatology*, 16–17.

Spirit as Wind and Breath

34:13–15).[9] The withdrawal of the Spirit indicates that the essence of life has subsided and departed. God as Spirit is the giver of life, encompassing the capability to bring the dead back to life.

The Spirit of God is at work in creation (Ps 33:6). Creation emerges out of the powers and vibrations of God's Holy Spirit. The Spirit hovers over the Earth and gives life. The Spirit moves, and life springs forward. This is evident when one studies atoms and recognizes that the electron shells of atoms are in constant vibration, taking form as a kinetic wave. The early Greek philosophers discovered this, subsequent to Heraclitus's statement that "ever-newer waters flow on those who step into the same rivers." Even Plato repeated this idea in his dialogue, *Cratylus*. In addition, the Spirit of God works through providence (Job 10:12) and redemption (Ezek 37:1).[10]

Pneuma refers to the breath of life (Luke 8:55; Acts 17:25; Rev 11:11; 13:15). In the Gospel of John, as noted earlier, the risen Christ is said to breathe upon his disciples as they were gathered together and thus transmitted to them the Holy Spirit (John 20:22).

In certain ways, we have unconsciously restricted how we view the Spirit and how we understand the movement and presence of the Spirit. Thus, we need to be reminded that it is the Spirit that breathes into us. We need it to give us life. We need to be perceptive to how breath moves in us and blows where it wishes.

The divine within us is not exactly our own literal breath, but breath that is provided to offer a possible analogue to what we mean when we speak of the human "soul" or "spirit." Breath is enlivening; it sustains us even when we become ignorant to it and ultimately forget it. Breath is vital to our individual existence, and yet it is not "ours," for we share the vital presence of breath with all that lives, including God.[11]

People of many traditions speak of the breath of life as God-given or even as God-within. There is something sacred about that which enlivens us and breathes in us. The *ruach* of a person is the God-given breath of life. As it is written in Job, "The spirit of God has made me, and the breath of the Almighty gives me life. . . . If he should take back his spirit to himself, and gather to himself his breath, all flesh would perish together, and all mortals return to dust" (Job 33:4). In many religious traditions, breath is a primary

---

9. Pannenberg, *Systematic Theology*, 76–77.
10. Pungur, *Theology Interpreted*, 83.
11. Eck, *Encountering God*, 122.

image for the divine presence within.[12] So, too, is *chi*, the breath and the Spirit of the divine that exists in all of us. It is what gives us life; in turn, we must recognize its power.

The Holy Spirit seeks to be embodied, and this is seen at Pentecost. The Holy Spirit comes down upon the people like a gust of wind and fire and fills them. The Spirit empowers the people to do things that are unexpected. This is the wonderful thing about the Spirit: it keeps us connected to God. God dwells in creation and in all of us, and our lives are fuller and more complete when we recognize God's presence in our lives. The incarnation means the Word embraced flesh.

In the West, there is a tendency to divorce the Spirit from the body, invariably elevating the former and denigrating the latter. A disembodied spirit does not exist in biblical narratives, only a Spirit who descends on bodies in creation.[13] We are made of both Spirit and body.

Breath Is Life

When we think about life, we often associate it with breath. This essential sign of life indicates to us that there is energy in existence. In the same way that breath is a signal for life, the Hebrew *ruach* is portrayed as a signal of a life-giving Spirit in the Old Testament.

The Old Testament shows the Spirit as the divine power that creates, sustains, and renews life (Gen 1:2; Ps 33:6). The Spirit is a life-giving Spirit of God. This power of the Spirit is found in the prophetic books of Isaiah, Ezekiel, and Joel. In the book of Ezekiel, we find the story of the dry bones.

> The hand of the Lord came upon me, and he brought me out by the spirit of the Lord and set me down in the middle of a valley; it was full of bones. He led me all around them; there were very many lying in the valley, and they were very dry. He said to me, "Mortal, can these bones live?" I answered, "O Lord God, you know." Then he said to me "Prophesy to these bones, and say to them: O dry bones, hear the word of the Lord. Thus says the Lord God to these bones: I will cause breath to enter you, and you shall live. I will lay sinews on you, and will cause flesh to come upon you, and cover you with skin, and put breath in you, and you shall live; and you shall know that I am the Lord. So I prophesied as I had been

---

12. Eck, *Encountering God*, 123.
13. Jensen, "Discerning the Spirit," 1–2.

Spirit as Wind and Breath

> commanded; and as I prophesied, suddenly there was a noise, a rattling, and the bones came together, bone to its bone. I looked, and there were sinews on them, and flesh had come upon them, and skin had covered them; but there was no breath in them.' Then he said to me, "Prophesy to the breath, prophesy, mortal, and say to the breath: Thus says the Lord God: Come from the four winds, O breath, and breathe upon these slain, that they may live." I prophesied as he commanded me, and the breath came into them, and they lived, and stood on their feet, a vast multitude. (Ezek 37:1–10)

This passage from Ezekiel provides hope to those who experience dryness, hopelessness, and a lack of will to live. In the depths of the dryness and difficulties of our lives, we are given hope that we can turn to God at any time, who is the life-giving Spirit. The Spirit can give power, strength, and love to those who come before God and can give life to dry bones.

The creative power of God is the transcendent side of *ruach*. *Ruach* is present in everything, sustaining all life. The trees and the birds that we see cannot be God, but they suggest that God is present within creation and thereby within all of us. This presence of God is possible through the Spirit as it permeates all things.

Just as there was power in the wind that the Israelites experienced in the desert and through the Red Sea, there is also power in the valley of the dry bones. This is the power of the Spirit of God that moves and gives full life. God, as the life-giving Spirit, is the complete source of all life and strength. In Psalm 36:9, God is called the well of life.

We see other images of the well in the New Testament. In John 4:14, Jesus meets a Samaritan woman at the well. He tells the woman that he will give the water that wells up out of the fountain of eternal life. He links water to the life-giving source—not just in our earthly life but also an everlasting life that goes beyond the depths of our burials, our graves, or physical vestige. The image of the wellspring of life, the water that gives life to everything that is parched and dry, depicts the importance of how the Spirit can quench thirst. As the water of life, the Spirit gives life to the dying.[14] The Spirit is the giver of life, and it will bring back to life that which is dying.

A few years ago, I took my family to a conference in Brazil. There, we experienced the beautiful sun of the South Americas, which was a wonder in every sense of the word. It was immensely powerful, giving light to

---

14. Moltmann, *Source of Life*, 12.

historic streets and monuments of the nation while also proving to be a source of constant exhaustion. The heat was dry, and it was scorching.

For the first time in my life, I experienced what real thirst actually felt like. Not just a parched feeling in the throat that I feel usually after my daily runs or a long lecture. This was different. It was a deep, un-swallowable dryness that suffocated me and permeated my mouth, throat, and chest. One day, our family ventured in the mountains to view Christ the Redeemer. We were in line to see the monument. We waited forty-five minutes.

This proved to be the longest forty-five minutes I had felt in a long time. You just don't forget that heat. With no close shade, I quickly grew tired under the punishing rays of the sun. I remember thinking about one thing and one thing only: an ice-cold glass of water. I knew that once I had that one drink, I would feel momentary alleviation, some hope. But until I had that glass of water, I remained rendered weak and hopeless from the heat.

In many ways, the Spirit is life-giving. The Spirit as one who gives life and can quench the deepest thirst, the thirst of our souls and our bodies.

It is important to remember the association of the Spirit with wisdom, as in Deuteronomy 34:9, where Moses passes the Spirit of wisdom onto Joshua, somewhat akin to Jesus' passing the Holy Spirit onto his disciples in John 20:22. The Spirit as wisdom continues to guide God's chosen people so that they can be led to make the right decisions.

Breath evokes the sense of the intimacy and presence of the Spirit. *Ruach* is the breath of life and the power to live (Eccl 3:21; 12:7). In the Hebrew Bible, life-sustaining breath is a result of the divine. It is the creative power of Yahweh who bestowed life into creation (Job 27:3; 33:4; Ps 104:29–30; Zech 12:1); thus, the creativity of God is linked by breath to creation. It is the creative act of God that brings all things into existence and co-existence. "This breath is the essence of life" (Gen 6:17), and without it, is death. This is significant as the Spirit is derived from one source—God.

Breath is a vital element to all living beings. In Genesis 2, God formed man from the dust of the ground and breathed the breath (*ruach*) of life into his nostrils. With that breath, he became alive. When the divine Spirit disappears from the living creature, only dust is left: "For you are dust, and to dust you shall return" (Gen 3:19); "If he should take back his spirit to himself, and gather to himself his breath, all flesh would perish together, and all mortals return to dust" (Job 34:14–15). God's *ruach* sustains the being of the universe and energizes its processes. God is constantly present and breathes with the breath of the world.[15]

Breathing Exercises and Prayer

Breath is the invisible icon of the divine. In breath-centered meditation, one rests the mind in the breath, returning again and again to the breath as the mind wanders. The breath draws one back to awareness and presence, bringing the self back to cohesive connection. In Christian meditation, it is the breath that draws one to the awareness of God. To speak of our human breath is a reminder of God's presence. It also becomes a way for us to be drawn toward God's presence at any time and place. Breath is like an invisible thread connecting God and us.[16] Breath is always with us. Remembering the breath and returning to the breath becomes a way of remembering, and it returns us back to God's embrace and presence.[17] As seekers, it becomes necessary to be aware of this breath, which draws us to the divine.

Creation

God's Spirit is within us and all of creation as it breathes through all things. We cannot allow dualistic ideas to make us think that the Spirit and our material world are separate. Just like particles and waves in light, we rely on the synergy of separate things to persist. We must recognize that the two are not mutually exclusive.

God's Spirit as breath and wind is continually renewing creation and preserves it from annihilation. In Genesis, God charges us to help with this task of preserving creation. "Then God said, 'Let us make humankind in our image, according to our likeness; and let them have dominion over the fish of the sea, and over the birds of the air, and over the cattle, and over all the wild animals of the earth, and over every creeping thing that creeps upon the earth'" (Gen 1:26–27). Oftentimes, we forget this charge and neglect our own responsibility in preserving God's creation. It is not a one-time act. It is continuous action towards preservation, a daily task that we need to be constantly practiced and taught to others.

---

15. Wright, *New Heavens, New Earth*, 16.
16. Eck, *Encountering God*, 122.
17. Eck, *Encountering God*, 128.

The creation story in the Priestly[18] writing talks about the *ruach Elohim*, which "vibrated" over the chaos (Gen 1:2). God creates everything through the Word as God speaks in the creative energies of the *ruach*. All creatures come to life through the one same *ruach*, and it is this that constitutes the community of creation.

The Spirit Within

God's enlivening presence within us gives us life. The Holy Spirit makes us "spiritually" alive. It inspires and strengthens us and gives us aspirations, inspirations, and intuitions. It opens us to new truths and enables us to integrate these truths into our minds and lives. God's presence also assures us of divine acceptance and companionship as it guides us and binds us to one another. We invoke the presence of God by saying, "Come, Holy Spirit, come." It expresses our hope that the universal presence of God will become more real to us. We want the Spirit to open us to its presence so we may be transformed. We believe that this openness to God's transforming presence will make us truly alive,[19] awakening the side of our being which can be neglected.

We are a habitation of a God who also inhabits all created things. We are a dwelling place of Christ crucified, who lived and died for the sake of abundant life for all.[20] The mystery of creation "is the indwelling of God within it."[21] The creatures God indwells are not limited to the human. Luther insisted that God and Christ are present not only in human beings but also in all created things.

God lives in us so that we can work for justice and repair broken relationships.

Chi reminds us that God and God's Spirit is always within us. We are the holy temples of God, and this knowledge should make all the difference in how we treat ourselves, others, and nature.

---

18. According to a major scholarly theory about the sources of the Torah, the different stories in Genesis come from an old source, called Yahwist (c. 950 BCE), and a newer source, called Priestly (c. 550 BCE). These and two other sources were merged, during the Babylonian exile, to create the first four books of the Torah.

19. Cobb Jr., "Holy Spirit and the Present Age," 149.

20. Moe-Lobeda, *Healing a Broken World*, 84.

21. Moe-Lobeda, *Healing a Broken World*, 133.

Spirit as Wind and Breath

We are not separate from the Spirit; rather, we interconnect, making us one with the Spirit. This oneness of the Spirit brings healing, restores what has gone wrong, and mends broken relationships. As the Spirit of God resides in each of us, we reflect that to others around us.

The Spirit "dwells deeply within all that exists, energizing, animating, and sustaining everything in the process of being and becoming."[22] God's Spirit is always within us, giving us life and sustaining us throughout our lives. We are all the holy temples of God, and this knowledge can make all the difference in our relationships. By recognizing that God is within us, we will begin to treat ourselves, others, and nature with the deserved respect, love, and compassion.

Long before Christ was incarnated, the Spirit had always led people to a sense of holy mystery. We need to be much more discerning in distinguishing Western Christian ideology[23] and profound biblical truth. The Spirit energizes and empowers us "toward a fuller and deeper sense of our sacred humanity, as well as a deeper recognition of the sacred at work in every sphere of God's creation."[24] As our lives become transformed, we will become aware of the work of the Spirit within us.

The Spirit provides a reminder of God's presence in the world, working actively among us, in us, and through us as we pursue justice.[25] The Spirit transforms us and, in turn, leads us to transform the world. In the thought of many theologians and philosophers, the Spirit is immanent, willful, and moving rather than remote and stagnant. The Spirit blows and sweeps through the Earth, bringing forth the most powerful of transformations.

---

22. O'Murchu, *In the Beginning*, 96.

23. Influential nineteenth- and twentieth-century theologians such as Albrecht Ritschl, Ernst Troeltsch, and Adolf von Harnack have made the case that the teachings of Jesus and Paul were folded into the transcendentalist Greco-Roman Platonism and Stoicism by Greek and Latin church theologians, and that this influence has persisted, despite major thrusts away from those notions by Kierkegaard and Schleiermacher.

24. O'Murchu, *In the Beginning*, 100.

25. The Platonic ideal that separates the divine from the immediate persists even into our modern thinking. See Whitehead, *Process and Reality*, 209: "Plato found his permanences in a static, spiritual heaven, and his flux in the entanglement of his forms amid the fluent imperfections of the physical world."

Different Religions

If Yahweh's Spirit is present everywhere and experienced everywhere, could it be the same Spirit that is recognized in other cultures, but simply named differently? The Scriptures talk about how the Spirit will be poured out on "all flesh," on all kinds of people, both young and old, from all cultures and environments (Joel 2:28–29; Acts 2:17–18). The ministry of the Spirit is always particular and specific. God's Spirit is not a numinous power hovering above the cosmos but rather a person living and permeating through people in diverse life circumstances and contexts.[26] The Spirit of God is poured upon all people.

As we've already discovered, the Christian understanding of the Spirit is similar to the Asian understanding of *chi*, the power of life that interpenetrates all entities, including both animate and inanimate objects. This understanding of the Spirit mirrors the Taoist understanding of *chi* regarding animate and inanimate objects. There appears to be continuity between the Holy Spirit (the primordial *chi*), human spirit (substantial *chi*),[27] and people of varying cultures and backgrounds where the Spirit is articulated in different languages.

The notion of a primordial is common in Taoism. Taoism's creation story speaks of an original, primordial oneness of the Tao, which is composed of energies.[28] Substantial spirit is that which is present in humans. Spirit is necessary to achieve calm, using the techniques of Taoism, Confucianism, and Buddhism.[29] Spirit is a vital component of life.

So, what happened to the Holy Spirit in the 1960s Christian theology? Indigenous spiritualities, which are generally Earth-centered and feminine, were presented and examined as an alternative model to the theologies of colonial Christianity. Eco-theology recognized and affirmed a cosmic Spirit as an expression of the creative work of God in the world.[30] A new, global theological perspective challenged the predominance of the notion that the Spirit—that aspect of the divine which works in the world—could only work for Christians. There was an increasing acknowledgment that the Spirit is at work around the world in all cultures and all peoples. The

---

26. Karkkainen, *Pneumatology*, 139.
27. Yun, "Pneumatological Perspectives on World Religions," 165.
28. For more on this discussion, see Wong, *Being Taoist*.
29. Wong, *Being Taoist*, loc. 352.
30. Chung, "Ecology, Feminism," 175–78.

Spirit as Wind and Breath

Breath of God (*Ruach Ha Kodesh* in Hebrew, *Spiritus Sanctus* in Latin) is synonymous with the power of Spirit. A similar idea is expressed in the holy Scripture of Islam, the *Qur'an* (Koran). The words *nafas*, meaning Allah's own breath, and *ruh*, meaning Allah's own soul, "are used to mean the human breath and human soul-confirming the fact that we are originally from Allah."[31]

Climate Change

Climate change affects everyone. However, within less developed, economically vulnerable regions, the populace is subject to increased destructive effects of wasteful lifestyles in first world countries. Women are at a particularly higher risk because they make up the majority of the world's poor and tend to be more dependent on natural resources for their livelihood and survival. In the exploited world, poor women are often the primary caregivers of their families and hence play an important role in securing their household with water, food, and fuel. In times of drought, women must walk farther and spend more time collecting water. In pursuit of supporting their families, countless young women are obligated to drop out of school and spend their time helping their households, continuing a cycle of poverty and gender inequity.[32] As poor women in the global South often have limited access to education, they also have limited choices of employment and stifled incomes. They are the ones most vulnerable when rural families are forced to migrate due to rising sea levels, desertification, earthquakes, and cyclones as the affect of climate change proliferates.

Women are further at increased risk because of the lack of independence and decision-making power, which significantly constrains their ability to cope with the consequences of climate change. As women are overwhelmingly underrepresented in community politics, their breadth of influence is marginal through politicized institutions. They are given little influence over community strategies in adapting to changing weather patterns in ways that support their priorities and rights. Thus, many

---

31. Cohen, *Way of Qigong*, 23.

32. The connections between the effects of climate change on poor women are widely reported. See, for instance, WHO, *Gender, Climate Change and Health*; UNFPA, *State of the World Population*. A very helpful documentary is *Weathering Change*, a movie by Population Action International that documents stories about climate and family from women around the world. See www.weatheringchange.org

environmental, grassroots movements neither originated with women nor with the intention to heed to needs of the most at-risk women or how they can be educated and empowered to impose themselves as powerful voices in their communities.[33]

Our neglect of the environment has led to some of the most catastrophic events on Earth. With climate change, we are reaching the brink. The present 2-degree increment in temperatures will have a devastating effect on sea levels, as scientists forewarn us of the effects that will be unleashed on low-lying island nations, causing them to be submerged deeper under water. Droughts and storms will continue to intensify, and a third of Earth's species will be at risk of extinction. It is a dangerous threshold to cross. If the ice caps melt, which is actively occurring, the sea levels will increase, taking away the homes and structural systems of millions of people.

Living as Christians, we remember that God as Spirit is in our midst, and God's presence in our daily lives assures us of our responsibility to preserve and be good stewards of all created things. God as *ruach* gives life to every living thing on this planet, and we have no right to destroy, conquer, exploit, or abolish whatever we wish for to advance our personal gain.

The *ruach* of God remains with, suffers with, and redeems the beloved creation. The biblical story of creation and fall from grace (Gen 1–3) cast forward in thought to this end or redemption, which all suffering creatures wait for with longing (Rom 8:19ff). As Jürgen Moltmann so eloquently observes:

> Anyone who wants to talk about God's activity in the world now, in the present, must have this purpose in mind: God preserves those he has created for their perfecting. His preservation of creation in itself already prepares for that perfecting. Every act that preserves creation from annihilation is an act of hope for its future.[34]

This is the way God loves those he has created, enticing them to turn back from death to life and to return home to God's eternal kin-dom. If we see the wonder of creation as a communication of God's creative love, then in the wonder of creation's preservation, we will see the inexhaustible power of that love. In these things, God's hope for the future finds expression.

Creation's history of suffering is God's history of suffering, too. The history of the return to life of created beings is a history of God's joy in that

---

33. See Kim and Koster, *Planetary Solidarity*.
34. Moltmann, *Source of Life*, 119.

Spirit as Wind and Breath

which he has created. For through God's immanent Spirit, God participates in the fate of what is created. In the sighs and groans of suffering creation, God's Spirit itself sighs and calls for redemption. God, who through God's indwelling Spirit suffers with those God has created, is the firm hope of created human beings. This hope is our assurance that the beings God has created have not been forsaken by their Creator.[35] The Spirit of God will not neglect us but will be with us always. God's indwelling Spirit offers hope, love, and peace while carrying on with the work of creation and salvation.

The Spirit is in the breath and wind, and it permeates all of creation. The Spirit calls us to action to make our world a more just place. The Spirit as breath unites people, bringing to them a fruitful, life-sustaining world into being. The Spirit as the breath of life convicts us of our sinful ways of living and pushes us towards climate justice. The Spirit as breath shows us the need to eliminate *han* from the Earth. The Spirit helps us envision ways of addressing the problem of climate change. The Earth is breaking, it is crying out to be healed, and the Spirit as wind and breath is diverting the course away from humanity's destruction.

Concluding Thoughts

Spirit is wind and breath. Wind and breath are part of life, and without them there is no life. Wind allows seeds to fall and plants to grow. Pollen is blown in the wind to give birth to new flowers that bud and create new life. The wind refreshes us on a hot summer day, cooling the moisture that perspires, giving us a gust of momentary ease and eventual hope.

These two vital elements, wind and breath, are what keep us alive and keep us thriving. They are essential. If we understand the essential aspect of the Spirit and its presence as wind and breath in the same way, we will come to recognize the reality of changes that the Spirit brings into our lives. We will become privy to the Spirit's life-giving power and the daily renewal that it generates with each new breath and each fresh breeze. The Spirit exhibits to us that there is *han* or suffering in this world. This chapter explored the ecological state of our world, and the present injustices that are perpetuated as our society has normalized and glorified wasteful lifestyles and the cultivation of material goods.

---

35. Moltmann, *Source of Life*, 119–20.

CHAPTER 4

Spirit as Vibration

My Church Upbringing

My upbringing in the church is a dynamic mix of Pentecostal, Baptist, Missionary Alliance, and Presbyterian influences. It is an unlikely breed of denominations, but it has made a profound impact on my Christianity, especially on my understanding of the Holy Spirit.

I grew up in the small city of London, Ontario, which was a few hours west of Toronto. As a child, I attended worship services in congregations within a myriad of denominations as my father felt that it was necessary and beneficial to expose me and my sister to as many non-Korean churches as possible. I spoke Korean at home and English at school, but my English proved to be of lower quality than my father's inflated expectations. It was confusing in the beginning, switching between languages, environments, and polarizing cultures. It established what would be an insecure foundation for my identity, but that confusion ultimately proved to come to my advantage later on.

Other than home and school, church became the other common dwelling place. It was an accessible place to learn English and was generally free of any cost. As an immigrant, my father insisted that his daughters grew up with an accurate understanding of Western culture, so he acculturated us to this strangely foreign world by taking us to the non-Korean church services throughout the week. This meant that not only were we immersing ourselves in as many "English classes" as we could attend, but we were also spending additional time in the church. After our regular Korean

Spirit as Vibration

Presbyterian Church's Sunday service, he took us to a Sunday night Baptist service, a Wednesday night Baptist service, and a Friday night Missionary Alliance Bible Study and youth group. As a young girl, my week was exhaustingly full of church events. My life at that time was comprised of the only two things I knew, school and church.

My parents tried to get out of London, Ontario, on various weekends in the limited free time they had, and they looked forward to going to Toronto and Detroit to attend revival services. These were not the rigorously insipid Presbyterian services that I attended on Sundays, nor the always-friendly, all-smiles Baptist services I attended on Wednesday and Sunday nights. These revivals were quite literally "out of this world" experiences, and it would be an understatement to say that they were frightening. I saw things that I had never seen in any of my time at the other churches, but it was during these services that I first witnessed the effects of the Holy Spirit.

These Pentecostal revival services were scarily visceral for an eight-year-old. They were "baptism by fire" encounters. All of the adults would gather together in a private back room for several hours. The only hint as to what they were doing was translated through muffled sounds of manic yelling, laughing, shouting, screaming, and crying. As the adults were caught up in the Spirit, the kids were in another area of the church. Opposed to the obscured grown-up activities, us children were doing kid stuff—yelling at one another, playing tag and hide-and-go-seek. We were a tireless and rambunctious group, but even in our own noisiness, I could not help but to hear the cries of worship in the closed room.

One day, my curiosity got the better of me. While I was playing games outside with the other kids, I remember feeling the creeping impulse to see what was actually going on in that private room where my parents were. I could no longer leave it to mystery, and I discreetly snuck out, walking inside through the narrow corridors of the church, getting closer to the sounds. Once I reached the door, I pushed it so lightly, as if to test my strength to see if I could actually do it.

It cracked open, revealing a sliver of the interior, and what I saw was a jarring scene indeed: familiar faces in unfamiliar states of frenzied devoutness. Some threw their arms up with tears streaming down their faces, praying and crying out to God. Some lay on the floor, weeping and shaking uncontrollably. My eyes darted across to fanatical dancing, while others remained completely silent and shook so violently that they fell over. My ears sharpened to the noises of alien languages—"speaking in tongues"—and my body curled in fear. Finally, I glanced over at a man with a microphone at the front of the sanctuary. I couldn't decipher whether he was preaching or praying, but whatever he was doing, it seemed as if he was angry about it, as his screams pierced my naive little ears. To add to the symphony of sounds, I can recall the distant whisper of a piano playing in the background, as if the music was meant to calm the screams of the congregation and soothe my own shock.

What I saw, heard, and witnessed was not like my other worship experiences. Undeniably, I was frightened, but more than that, I was curious, more curious than before. I wanted to know why they had no control over their bodies and minds and ultimately, why they kept coming back. They seemed crazed, but when they left each time, they reverted back to the sanity and normalcy. What happened in that room that made these people behave in this way? Were they possessed or mentally unwell? I just could not understand. After I first peeked in the room, I remember trying to go back and play with my friends, but what was done was done—I could not stop myself from going back and looking. It was petrifying, but the fragment of mania kept me coming back. Later, when I came back another time to peek, my eyes were drawn to the back of the room. Illuminated in the yellow church light was my mother—she stood upright with her hands high above her head, eyes closed, with tears rolling down her face as she spoke in tongues.

I wondered what my mom and all the others were doing in the sanctuary, but I could not muster the courage to ask her or my father on the ride home. I was just glad that we were gone and that whatever happened in that sanctuary somehow made them feel better. It was strange because family car trips were usually a vehicle for intense family argument, but after those revival services, we always drove home in high spirits. During these rides home, I had conversations in my head with myself, thinking, "If my parents are involved with this and are happier as a result—it must be okay." Yet persisting in the back of my mind was the gnawing thought that this might be what Christianity is all about. Like Shakespeare's Hamlet approaching the vision of his father, I asked myself, was this the work of the Holy Spirit or was it some evil spirit that made people speak in tongues and move around as though they were possessed?

After this early exposure to Korean Pentecostal Christianity, I felt that I did not want anything to do with the Holy Spirit. This childhood experience felt threatening and invasive, and I thought that if this was what the Holy Spirit was like, I should simply move on to another religion.

These revivals occurred every four months. In between, I experienced the Holy Spirit within my Korean Presbyterian church in a more restrained manner: through prayer and my own youth Bible study. I was shown what Scripture had to say about the Holy Spirit, and unlike the revival services, these encounters with the Holy Spirit were comforting and more sensible to me, so I stayed in the church.

Comforting Spirit or Terrifying Fire?

As I matured through my early youth and developed my spiritual practice, I asked myself the same question over and over, "*Is this really the Holy Spirit?*"

The biblical understanding is that the Holy Spirit is life-giving and not fear-instilling. But my childhood experiences of the Holy Spirit were scary. They instilled in me a fear that if I called upon the Spirit, I would become "possessed" and fall into the same terrifying things that I saw through the chilling crack of the door.

How do we strike a balance between the church's long history of a stoic, comforting Spirit and the crazy, fanatical, hand-raising, and body-shaking understanding of the Spirit in the twentieth-century revival service?

Unfortunately, the church's history offers a limited perspective on the Holy Spirit. Pneumatology, or the study of the Holy Spirit, has been suffocatingly patriarchal. Pneumatology is rooted in the Greek word *pneuma*, which means breath, wind, energy, and life-giving spirit. This historically repressive pneumatology began with the early church fathers and continued to dominate our thought on the Holy Spirit up to the 1960s, when diverse and previously marginalized voices from around the world—Latin American, African, Asian, and women—began to emerge in theological discourse. Prior to this time, it was virtually impossible for those on the margins to embrace the antiquated understanding of Spirit.

A leading twentieth-century German theologian, Jürgen Moltmann, developed a liberation theology predicated on the view that God suffers with humanity and promises humanity a better future through the hope of the resurrection. Moltmann points out that Yahweh's *ruach* (Spirit or breath) is present in everything, which is constant with his *panentheism*, the theological belief that God is in all things (as distinct from *pantheism*, which holds that God *is* all things). Moltmann writes powerfully about how the passionate love of the Trinity overflows from its own bounds and spills over all of creation. It is God's Spirit that then embraces all of creation and suffuses it with God's love.

How can finite beings even imagine limiting God's presence and expression in God's creation and the created world? Furthermore, how can only a few experience God's wondrous presence in this world when God is all-encompassing? Understanding that the Spirit is universal, no matter what name and what religion, opens our minds and vastly extends our conception of personal spiritual horizons. This liberation can provoke fascinating explorations of the infinite God that we worship. It can reinstate the mysterious aspect of the Divine and also open possibilities of creativity, love, expansion, embracement, and wonder. The cosmic understanding of Spirit is all that and more, freeing up our view to one that allows for more extensive understandings of the Trinity.

We often put God in a neatly decorated box, with our own biases, ideas, concepts, and understandings that we impose upon the infinite God. We make God simple. We render our understanding of God as if God were an object, able to be molded and manipulated. Even worse, we imagine that we have other boxes to encase God, where God has no place. We feel that we know all that we need to know, that we have reached a point where all problems have been solved. But we need to widen our understanding. We need to challenge our preconceptions, even as it requires us to get out of our stagnated and comfortable states and explore the discomfort surrounding an ever-reforming image of the Creator that is, was, and ever will be.

Understanding that God's Spirit is everywhere and that other people from different religions, cultures, and traditions can experience it should be assurance to us that the Spirit is a comforting Spirit and not a terrifying one. God's Spirit is upon us all. We must put a positive and inclusive approach to studying the Scriptures and trying to understand the Spirit into practice. We are all created in the image of God, whether we are Christian or Buddhist, refugee or indigenous, woman or man.

Shekinah, Spirit, and the Bible

The rabbinic literature uses the word *Shekinah* to describe the presence of God. The Jewish rabbis coined this extra-biblical expression, a Hebrew word that means "he caused to dwell." Although the word is not found in the Old Testament, its concept certainly is. *Shekinah* developed out of cultic language and originally meant God's tabernacle or tent, God's "dwelling" among God's people, first in the transportable ark and then in the temple, where God finds "rest." The *Shekinah* is the presence of God. It is God's special, willed, and promised presence in the world. The *Shekinah* is God, present at a particular place and at a particular time.[1]

Shekinah as the presence of God is life-giving. *Shekinah* was with the Israelites and sustained them as they roamed around. The *Shekinah* was experienced when the Israelites set out from Succoth in their escape from Egypt. There, the Lord appeared in a cloudy pillar in the day and a fiery pillar by night: "By day the LORD went ahead of them in a pillar of cloud to guide them on their way and by night in a pillar of fire to give them light so that they could travel by day or night. Neither the pillar of cloud by day nor the pillar of fire by night left its place in front of the people" (Exod 13:21–22).[2]

As the Exodus story progresses, God speaks to Moses out of the pillar of cloud, assuring him that God's presence would be with the Israelites (Exod 33:9). Verse 11 says God spoke to Moses "face to face" out of the cloud, but when Moses asked to see God's glory, God told him, "You cannot see My face; for no man shall see Me, and live" (Exod 33:20). God says that God will sanctify God's glory and will dwell among the children of Israel.[3] While God's physical presence cannot be seen, it can be felt unequivocally.

The visible manifestation of God's presence was not only available to the Israelites but also was seen by the Egyptians: "During the last watch of the night, the LORD looked down from the pillar of fire and cloud at the Egyptian army and threw it into confusion. He made the wheels of their chariots come off so that they had difficulty driving. And the Egyptians said, 'Let's get away from the Israelites! The LORD is fighting for them against Egypt'" (Exod 14:24–25). The presence of God's *Shekinah* glory was enough to convince the enemies that they should not go after the Israelites.

In the New Testament, Jesus Christ is the dwelling place of God's glory. Colossians 2:9 tells us that "in Christ all the fullness of the Deity lives in bodily form," causing Jesus to exclaim to Philip, "Anyone who has seen me has seen the Father" (John 14:9). In Christ, we see the visible manifestation of God in the second person of the Trinity. The divine Presence dwelled in a plain tent called the "tabernacle" before the Temple in Jerusalem was built,

---

1. Moltmann, *Spirit of Life*, 48.
2. Miller, *Skekinah Glory*, 36.
3. Miller, *Skekinah Glory*, 38.

just as the Presence dwelled in the relatively plain humanity of Jesus. The Spirit dwelling in Jesus was not still, but in constant motion, shifting like a huge wind upon the people that Jesus was with. After Jesus' resurrection, the presence of God is with us in the Spirit. The Spirit dwells on the Earth and is the divine presence.

In certain places in the New Testament, Scripture presents a gentle, comforting understanding of the Holy Spirit. It is through the Holy Spirit that people understood the presence of God. The Bible speaks of the Holy Spirit as wind, movement of air, breath, life-giving, comforter, and counsellor. The role of the Spirit in the New Testament becomes christological and ecclesial. At Pentecost, the Spirit came upon the people as tongues of fire and moved them. It moved upon the people, shook them up, and changed them. Could this be the movement of vibration of the Spirit? How does the Spirit move upon the people?

Thus, the presence of God is not merely still and calming. Both the Old Testament and New Testament illustrate that the presence of God involves movement. What is the cause of such movements? Certainly, it is the science of vibration that tells us that all things are in a state of movement.

The Science behind Vibrations

In high school, my favorite classes were math and science. I was the nerdy Asian girl, raising my hand too much and staying after the bell rang to chat with my teachers. While I was interested in all the sciences, biology was my preferred subject. I was fascinated with the miraculous breakdown of an object's composition, the profoundly complex system of cells and molecules working in a network to keep the body alive. I was eager to uncover the logistics and inner workings of human biology, getting to know myself in a whole other kind of way.

However, my passion for biology was nearly eclipsed by my frustration with the other science that I could not bring myself to be interested in—physics. I just couldn't grasp the conceptual ways calculations were done or why. I remember my physics teacher enthusiastically lecturing us about a car going at one speed on the slope of the hill at a certain angle and asking us how fast the car would go. To my mind, the car, the slope, the hill, the math, it all didn't make sense. I failed to grasp the question and subject as a whole, as I kept asking myself, "Who cares?"

Spirit as Vibration

Hindsight is a curious thing, and when I look back now, I wish I had been able to attain a fundamental understanding of basic physics. I believe it would have been helpful to my personal understanding of the Spirit, as I would like to view it from a perspective of pure calculated science.

Science has altered and revolutionized the way in which we see and understand the world around us, and I think it can also revolutionize the way we understand the Spirit of God. Up until Isaac Newton's famous work, *Opticks*, at the dawn of the seventeenth century, scientific evidence gave the impression that light was formed by particles. Just as Newton published his work, Robert Hooke proposed the wave theory of light. In this theory, light was made up of vibrations in a medium, like sound through the air or waves in a pond. This was supported by even more experimental evidence, such as the observation of the light spectrum's appearance as the arrestingly beautiful and mysterious rainbow.

In the twentieth century, after famous findings by Max Planck in the late nineteenth century, Albert Einstein used the particle notion of light to explain the photoelectric effect. This is where light, understood as vibrating waves, produces particles as it is struck against a metal surface. This signified the beginnings of acceptance that light acted as both a vibrating wave and as a particle—a *photon*—with a discrete charge. These scientific theories have revealed that there is certainly more than meets the eye. Things that we believed to be static are actually moving, making waves and effects on other things in their vicinity. It appears that light, sound, and matter are vibrating and, in turn, affect other vibrations everywhere in the world.

Similarly, when we examine the quantum-level building blocks within the atom, we recognize that the components of the atom, as minute as they are, are not like billiard balls or marbles; rather, they are more like active jump ropes, vibrating at different frequencies. All matter is vibrating, creating waves of energy such as light, sound, and movement. Nothing escapes vibration.

What was true of light became true of our familiar electrons, thought to be marbles spinning around the proton-neutron nucleus. In 1927, Erwin Schrödinger described electrons using wave equations. He presented the idea that electrons were vibrations rather than the previously thought billiard ball comparison. This was the dawn of modern quantum physics, which has completely reconstructed how we view our planet and the universe.

As we have examined vibrations, we have become aware that there are waves that the vibrations cause. We may know of color waves, sound waves, microwaves, or gamma rays, but scientists talk primarily about three types of waves: mechanical, matter, and electromagnetic. Since all things have energy and energy is transmitted by vibrations, all things participate in the basic wave mechanics of the universe.

Vibration and Culture

According to some, even our emotions and thoughts are vibrations that can affect our surrounding nature. Much like many other cultures, in Asian tradition, pregnant mothers are encouraged to be happy and stress-free. They believe that the negative thoughts of a mother can be passed on to their unborn child and that the happiness of pregnant women should be increased.

We don't just see this mentality in Asian cultures but throughout the world, the shared mentality that bad thoughts illicit bad things. Many feel that our thoughts can actually affect the outcome of certain events. This can be tied to wavelengths and vibrations. As all matter produces vibrations, it is important not to alter or suppress the wavelengths, which can ultimately generate greater difficulty and adverse situations.

The Japanese scientist Masaru Emoto photographed ice crystals to see if positive and negative speech had any effect on ice crystal formations. He found that positive speech and thoughts produced beautiful ice crystals, while negative thoughts and words produced misinformed and less "aesthetic" crystals. His experiment attempted to prove, in part, that speech, human emotion, and human consciousness affect things in our direct environment, particularly the molecular structure of water.

He hypothesized that as our bodies are made up of 70 percent water, if we say negative things to others, it may damage our internal bodies. When we really come down to it, the fetus is in an amniotic sac that contains the amniotic fluid. The sac is mostly water, which makes the Korean saying incredibly significant if Emoto's theory is true. If we take this one step further, we can see how positive vibrations and negative vibrations affect our surroundings and how this could have a ripple effect that impacts even those outside our small circle of conversation partners.

Spirit as Vibration

What is intelligible is musical! This idea even predates Plato, when Pythagoras discovered the relations between vibrations and music.[4] Many ancient mystery religions were based on arcane symbols, secret rites and ceremonies, and most importantly, music from song and instrument. With the pure tones of instruments being so close to the divine, one can only wonder, how are these tones produced? By vibrations of course.

Pythagoras discovered a remarkable number of characteristics of musical vibrations through his observations of tone from strings drawn out with various weights. Since the Greek world was already in possession of sophisticated knowledge in astronomy and mathematical relations between the seasons and eclipses, Pythagoras's inspiration of linking musical vibrations to the movement of celestial objects seemed natural. From this association, we arrive at the expression "The Music of the Spheres."[5]

What makes this vibratory theory close to our sense of spirituality is that from early times, just as with the early Taoist thinkers and their theories on harmony (see above), these relations were believed to be metaphysical.[6] In that way, the spiritual became known to us through the familiar vibrations we sense, whose primary action occurs in the spiritual realm. Employing this lens, we can rethink and continue to reimagine our understanding of the Holy Spirit.

Vibration in Popular Culture

The iconic Beach Boys song "Good Vibrations" was released in 1966 and remains a long-standing triumph in contemporary music history.[7] The song was composed by Brian Wilson, who recounts how his mother explained to

---

4. Guthrie, *Pythagorean Sourcebook and Library*, loc. 386.

5. Guthrie, *Pythagorean Sourcebook and Library*, loc. 440.

6. For our purposes, the study of metaphysics is the study of things we cannot, in principle, perceive with our five senses, because it deals with things we commonly describe as transcendental. The simplest example of a metaphysical finding is the transcendental moral law, "Thou shall not kill." In ancient times, when the Greeks could not measure, see, or know how vibrations were related to sound, they became transcendental properties. Much later, high speed cameras grounded those phenomena in the observable and not the metaphysical.

7. Some of this discussion on vibration and popular culture was developed through a lively discussion with Thomas Swan.

him as a child that dogs will sometimes bark at people in response to that person's bad vibrations.[8]

People seldom recognize that vibrations surround them, but may be aware of vibrations in their personal relationships. We can recognize that vibrations reverberate between one another, and those who give off "good vibrations" often gain positive responses from others, while those who emit bad vibrations will receive negative responses.

These "good" or "bad" vibrations are an integral part in determining whom we like and, conversely, whom we dislike. Naturally, we move towards those who emit good vibrations, especially those who resonate with our own vibrations. This is embodied in the axiom "like attracts like."

Furthermore, we talk about the "butterfly effect," the belief that even the smallest changes, like the flapping of butterfly wings, can produce an impact on monumental activities that are seemingly unrelated, like a storm halfway across the world. As such, this is not limited to the mere butterfly wing, but is also connected to the complexities of life on Earth: animals, plants, and people. Such a small thing, like a differing or unexpected form of vibration, can set off an entirely new course of action, manifested into altered results for humanity. Vibration is perhaps one of the most subtle yet powerful agents that can elicit the greatest of changes.

In C. S. Lewis's Narnia series, for instance, the great lion Aslan brought the world of Narnia and the creatures within it into existence through singing—that is, through the vibrations of sounds and musical notes. Surely, Lewis was purposely invoking the Genesis account of creation: "And God said, 'Let there be light' and there was light."

And so, there are sound waves or vibrations that elicit creation. Aslan's way of creation may not be too far-fetched from our own Christian biblical creation story. As sound waves affect the world, perhaps it is sound waves, or the "word of God," that ignited the world into being. Perhaps it is the Spirit's vibration that gave birth to the universe.

Spirit in Hinduism

Words of blessings and of curses have generally always been taken seriously by devout Hindus. Mantras, which are words or sounds repeated to aid concentration in meditation, are common practices within Hinduism. The mantra, used in connection with the Vedic sacrifice, is believed to work

---

8. Badman, *Beach Boys*, 117.

Spirit as Vibration

without fail. The Word, which is a series of vibrations, is a power that makes the gods subject to the will of humanity. "Brahman is the word" and the Brahmin, its keeper and Lord.

Speech itself was addressed as a deity in the Rigveda. In Hinduism, the body of a divinity was considered to consist of mantras that are identical with cosmic processes. The mantras could be said to originate in the consciousness of the eternal. A mantra can only take a devotee as high as the originator of the mantra. The mantras are a series of vibrations and sounds that come forth from human beings. The link of the concept of vibration to religious practice is a significant find, which shows that the concept of the Spirit cannot be limited to Christianity. In Hinduism, no sacrifice can be performed without the vocal expression of words. Tantric Hinduism operated with esoteric syllables that were meaningless for the non-initiate but full of significance and power for the one who had received dīkṣā.[9]

The most famous of all mantras is *OM (AUM)* also called *prāṇava*, which is a sacred sound and spiritual symbol in Hinduism. A mantra need not have an intelligible word meaning; it is the sound equivalent of reality and a medium by which a transcendent reality is reached. OM is not a concept of something; rather, it is the Supreme Being in the form of sound. It is the primeval sound, the medium between spiritual brahman and the concrete material world. The *Chāndogya Upaniṣad* calls OM the "all-word." Through the identification of important concepts and beings, the mantra OM is filled with concepts and meaning. The recitation of OM on the one hand reduces all beings into the nothing of OM, "the image of the supreme reality." On the other hand, the recitation makes OM itself meaningful without identifying it with any particular being. The *Māṇḍūkya Upaniṣad* identified AUM with the four stages of consciousness: *A* stands for the waking state, *U* for dream, *M* for deep sleep. AUM, in its totality, corresponds to the transcendent state. OM stands at the beginning of every hymn, every religious action, and every recitation of a sacred text. With OM, everything finds its conclusion.[10]

As we have observed, the Christian Bible begins with God speaking and creating the world. Speaking is a form of vibration, and it is through this act that God's presence is felt in the world. God's voice as vibration created the world that we live in.

---

9. Klostermaier, *Survey of Hinduism*, 56.
10. Klostermaier, *Survey of Hinduism*, 57.

Since the sacred texts themselves have the quality of mantras, the opinion could develop that it is ultimately unimportant whether their meaning is understood or not. Many Brahmins who traditionally function at the occasions where the recitation of Vedic mantras is required do not really understand their meaning. The blessing derived from Scripture does not depend on its comprehension: "The glorious and holy *Bhāgavata* confers long life, freedom from disease, and good health. One who recites it or listens to it is freed from all sins."[11]

The whole life of a Hindu is enveloped in mantras. The conception of a child is supposed to be accompanied by the recitation of mantras; mantras are spoken over the expectant mother before birth; birth itself, name giving, initiation and marriage, purification and temple visits, death, and cremation all have to be performed with mantras. At the time of initiation, ascetics receive a personal mantra, whispered into the ear by the guru. This will be their mantra through which they distinguish themselves from all the others: it is a name that nobody knows but the devotee and master. They are not permitted to divulge this secret word unless they themselves have to give *dīkṣa* to their disciples. Many Hindus carry mantras written on tiny pieces of paper in small capsules of copper, silver, or gold, fastened to arms, legs, or necks to protect themselves from certain illnesses or as a safeguard against the evil eye.[12]

The understanding of Scripture as mantra should neither obscure the importance of the understandable content nor the tremendous effort of countless generations of Hindus who derive meaning from it and build up a coherent system of philosophical religious thoughts. The desire for comprehension led to the elaboration of the *sutras*, in which the essentials of certain branches of knowledge are condensed and systematized.[13] The importance of the word and the vibration that happens when the word is spoken is found in different religious experiences and understandings. We cannot underestimate the significance of the similarities that occur between different religions. The similarities reveal the universality of the divine in our world. With this newfound understanding, we can try to work towards a more peaceful, non-disruptive, and crucial concept of the Spirit that exists in different religions.

---

11. Klostermaier, *Survey of Hinduism*, 57.
12. Klostermaier, *Survey of Hinduism*, 58.
13. Klostermaier, *Survey of Hinduism*, 58.

Spirit as Vibration
Holy Spirit Vibration

The proposed notion that God is in all things and that all things move and vibrate has opened up our understanding of the Spirit. The Spirit is alive and is the mover of all living things. Everything that is alive—plants, cells, animals, and human beings—moves.

As I reflect on praying, I am able to perceive an intimate connection between prayer, vibration, and Spirit. Prayers are vibrations from our lips, our hearts, and our minds. If positive thoughts affect us and the world around us, perhaps this is also a fragment to our understanding of how prayer works. People have always stated that prayer elicits changes in us and not God, who changes the course of our lives.

When I think of midwives and doulas helping with child birth, some of them use positive thinking and meditation to help with the birthing process. I have always dreamed of participating in such birthing practices, but with my low pain tolerance, skepticism, and acceptance that my three kids are probably enough, I know that I will not be able to try such a process. But according to those I know who have, it seems to be effective. This goes to show the power of vibrations and its direct implications on human lives.

As we pray "come Holy Spirit, come," we want the Spirit to come into our lives, reside in our lives, and change our lives. We cannot be the same as yesterday or today, but we change continuously for the better.

As individuals, we also work together to make changes in our society. We want the most pressing social concerns—issues that regard the minority or unfortunate—to be at the forefront of discussion so that we can work towards making proactive change. We want to flourish in our task of doing this work to also inspire others to follow suit.

Vibration is a unique perspective in which we can come to understand the Holy Spirit. This understanding of God as the Spirit that vibrates through the Earth reminds us with great clarity that God has presence on the Earth, in ourselves, and in the universe.

We have all likely been around a drummer playing and felt the reverberation in the whole room. We hear it and we feel it, and this drum of life becomes the composer of the beat of life. The vibrations connect us to each other.

Vibration is the oscillation of the parts of a fluid or an elastic solid whose equilibrium has been disturbed or affected by an electromagnetic wave. It is a person's emotional state, the atmosphere of a place, or the associations of an object as communicated to and felt by others. Vibration is a mechanical phenomenon whereby oscillations occur around an equilibrium point. In this way, vibration is "desirable."

For example, the motion of a tuning fork, the quivering reed in a wind instrument, or a buzzing cellphone are all necessary forms of vibration that facilitate the function of these objects. If the object fails to vibrate at the right frequency, then the wrong sound will be produced. Thus the correct vibration becomes necessary for the desired outcome.

The Spirit is vibration, as all things in our world have vibrations. This notion is an important concept to study as we try to navigate beyond the confines of Eurocentric and patriarchal models of understanding the Holy Spirit. This is another lens by which we can rethink or reimagine the Holy Spirit. Spirit as vibration moves us to take actions and initiatives now. The Spirit moves us into action as "vibration is action." Spirit as vibration accompanies us, empowers us, and stirs us to strive towards greater equity and justice.

As I witnessed the haze of madness in the Pentecostal revival services of my childhood, when I saw adults shaking, falling over, and dancing as they worshiped, it appeared as though the Spirit truly did move through people. It was not a silent and stagnant Spirit but rather a strong force of dynamic energy, urging people to make different actions.

At first, I saw the Holy Spirit's vibrations as being only bodily movements. Later, I saw them as something that moves us to work for change. The Spirit's vibrations reverberate in our bodies and push us to do something for the greater good. One of the things it motivates us to do is to work for social change and justice.

Spirit as Vibration Gives Life to Creation

Hovering over the universe, God has filled us with vibrations to energize and prompt progressive change. In the creation story in Genesis, the Spirit vibrated and gave birth to new things. "When you send your Spirit, they are created and you renew the face of the earth" (Ps 104:30). The life of all things and the breath of all people are in the hands of the Spirit. Job 12:10 states, "In his hand is the life of every living thing and the breath of every human being." All created matter vibrates, as created matter is never static. As living things vibrate, we are reminded that the Spirit initiated this vibration and has allowed all created things to vibrate.

Spirit as Vibration

Luke 21:33 states, "Heaven and earth will pass away but my words will never pass away." This is denotative of acknowledging the infinite. If God's words last forever and we understand God to be the infinite, then we must understand that God and the Word are same. The vibrations that come out of God's words are infinite. It is an infinite vibration.

The creation account in Genesis 1 reminds us that God is the creator of all things. God has wonderfully and magnificently created this world. We need to be constantly mindful of this and not destroy what God has created by our personal weakness for material gain, for everything that God created is good.

Ruach and the biblical concept of *ruach Elohim* (the breath of God) is described in terms of life-giving potential, preferring everything that prizes life over death.[14] God is the life-giving Spirit, and *ruach* denotes the life-force of the individual.

Judges 15:19 reads, "So God split open the hollow place that is at Lehi, and water came from it. When he drank, his spirit returned, and he revived." Numbers 16:22 states, "They fell on their faces and said, 'O God, the God of the spirits of all flesh, shall one sin and you become angry with the whole congregation?'" God is the only one who gives the life-force and protects it. God is the ultimate source of life and the one who sustains life.

God is called the fountain of life in Psalm 36:9. Jesus tells a Samaritan woman that he will give her water that will be like a spring gushing to eternal life (John 4:14). The image of water as the fountain or spring of life points to the effect of the Spirit. As water gives life, the Spirit transforms what is dying and withered into something living and fertile. The Spirit restores, renews, and sustains life.[15]

Creation only exists and lives through the presence of the divine Spirit. God constantly strengthens creation by giving *ruach* to it. Life depends on breath, and to breathe is to live by God's grace. As God breathes the breath of life, God will bring creation to life. Creation takes place by the powers and energies of God's own Spirit. It is the Spirit which bridges the gap between the Creator and the creature.

Created in God's image, the human creature creates and thus participates in Divine creativity. This does not make human creativity divine but rather brings the human creature into the sphere of the Spirit's power.[16]

---

14. O'Murchu, *In the Beginning*, 44.
15. Kim, *Holy Spirit, Chi, and the Other*, 44.
16. Kim, *Holy Spirit, Chi, and the Other*, 44.

As humanity recognizes that God is in all things, perhaps we will raise a stronger sense of responsibility and initiative to take care of the Earth and all the things that inhabit it. This understanding may allow us to show more reverence for our planet and to care for it in a manner befitting its sacredness. We are commanded to do no less.

We experience God's love in this creative orchestra that we live within and witness on a daily basis. We need to allow the movement of God's Spirit as a vibration to infuse our lives. We need to allow the creative power of the Spirit to vibrate through us, move within us, and guide our lives.

As we become too anthropocentric and increasingly centered on the distractions in our daily lives, we fail to see the redemptive love in everything we experience. If we can begin to open ourselves up to the possibility that others also hold wisdom and truth about God, we can work towards a new harmony, a new heaven, and a new Earth, achievable by the Spirit's vibration. Perhaps the Eastern tradition and culture has something to offer to Western theology, a widening not only of our minds but also of our hearts. If we are to survive in this world, then this is what we need to do.

Vibration and Climate Change

Climate change affects us all. Whether we are old or young, Latino or Asian, rich or poor, climate change will drastically affect how we live on this planet and how we survive. Climate change affects the poor disproportionately, even though it is the rich who are the predominant causers of climate change and climate-related issues. Since it is one of the most pressing issues of our time, the Spirit is urging us all to work for change and for justice.

Climate change is current. While many are under misguided notions that they are not being influenced by its effects right now, that judgment is gravely wrong. It is happening and it has been happening, so we need to move into immediate action to stop this hazardous lifestyle from destroying our planet. Taking action can mean changing our daily habits and ways of being, but it aims towards long-term plans on saving the planet from total and ultimate destruction. Theologians lead us to reimagine how we view the world. Sallie McFague provides three rules to abide by to live a more ecological and sustainable life: "In lay language, the ecological model claims that housemates abide by three rules: take only your share, clean up after yourselves, and keep the house in good repair for future occupants."[17] These

---

17. McFague, *Life Abundant*, 122.

rules are simple and easy to follow. But the perilous greed of humanity has made them nearly impossible to follow. If we were to abide by these simple rules, our existence would be cleaner, safer, and more sustainable.

We do not have more planets. We have only one. Therefore, we need to examine how we are living, the effects it has outside of us. We need to stop the perpetual overconsumption of natural resources for our short-term needs. Being a part of a wealthier nation, we feel more inclined to ignore the sufferings of those we don't see and continue to persist in our ignorant and hedonistic lifestyles. For instance, we have gotten so used to being in a state of comfort that we tend to blast the air conditioners in the summer and crank up the heat in the winter. This conditions us to necessitate comfortable temperature zones to the detriment of the planet. We are quickly using up all our resources and polluting the Earth for the sake of our own unrestrained need to have greater self-indulgence and satisfaction.

We need to heed the warning of both the scientists who predict catastrophes and the theologians who reveal the selfish ways of our life. Living by greed will lead to planetary economic shortages comparable to those suffered by the forgotten famines of biblical times. We need to stop "raping" the land and start nurturing it as wise stewards. As Christians, we have failed to do our part in becoming good stewards of the Earth and taking care of the planet that God created and gave us to protect, nurture, and conserve. We have neglected God's commands, choosing instead to exploit and deplete the Earth, as if we are the main players in this grand game. But unlike a game, we cannot "start over," and we will not be given a second chance.

Climate Issues

The *Report on Alternatives to Economic Globalization* does not provide a positive statement on the present condition of our Earth. It states, "Economic globalization is intrinsically harmful to the environment because it is based on ever-increasing consumption, exploitation of resources, and waste disposal problems."[18] This report brings to attention that companies, manufacturers, and consumers have continually input staggering stress on the Earth, manifesting into the problems we see today.

Some of the problems that the Earth is experiencing are the "depletion of the Earth's ozone layer; rising temperatures and freakish weather

18. Quoted in Gillet, *New Globalization*, 161.

patterns; rainforest destruction; the steady depletion of groundwater; the proliferation of nuclear waste; the pending mass production of genetically altered foodstuffs, seed, and animals; and other environmental threats constitute dire testimony to a basic incompatibility existing between the present global economic dynamic and the global environment."[19]

Sallie McFague reminds us that what we see in global warming is a prime example of negligible planetary management. *Ecumenical, ecological,* and *economical* all come from the same language root (from the word οἶκος, meaning house or home). The imagery of a house or home should generate a compassionate care for how we treat one another, the planet, and the rules that dictate the sharing of goods.

These three words describe the underlying rules whereby *all* of us, human and nonhuman, can live sustainably and justly in our house, planet Earth. Planetary economics is the equal sharing among basic needed resources in a fashion geared toward long-term sustainability. Justice and sustainability are the norms that guide the safe allocation of resources. This should also be kept in mind to prevent climate change[20] from destroying our planet. These three words—*ecumenical, ecological,* and *economical*—should rule everything that happens on our Earth. These are intertwined with one another and must not be forgotten.

We need to be mindful of the things that we put into the Earth, the ground, and the air. "Nitrous oxide comes especially from fertilizers, while herds of cattle and rice paddies emit methane gases. Carbon dioxide is now 30 percent higher in the earth's atmosphere than in preindustrial times; nitrous oxide is 19 percent higher."[21] Gases new to the Earth's atmosphere, chlorofluorocarbons and other chlorinated substances, are released by aerosol cans, air conditioners, and refrigerators. In the 1970s it began to become apparent that these chemicals were causing holes in the ozone layer. These holes allow ultraviolet rays to penetrate to the Earth, producing a variety of detrimental results. In the case of gases causing holes in the ozone layer, the damage is massive and difficult to grasp, as it is ongoing. These chemicals affect the Earth and its inhabitants on different levels, many of which are still being discovered.[22] The ways that these chemicals were and are continuing to cripple the Earth were once unknown or ignored. This was until

---

19. Gillet, *New Globalization*, 162.
20. McFague, *New Climate for Theology*, 37.
21. Ruether, *Integrating Ecofeminism, Globalization, and World Religions*, 11.
22. Kim, *Colonialism, Han, and the Transformative Spirit*, 48.

Spirit as Vibration

the damages were too great to ignore. This leads us to recognize that the way in which we live today and the pollutants that we emit on a daily basis are not always intentional and often damage the environment without our knowledge. Thus, we need to be aware and careful in all that we do.

Climate is the broadest, deepest, most intricate system on Earth, combining the effects of sunlight, rotation, revolutions, and tides to control temperature, wind, and ocean currents, affecting everything we know on Earth. It makes some places desirable and others undesirable, some places that were habitable turn completely uninhabitable. The quality of life for humans and other species depends on climate. Global warming illustrates just how vulnerable living creatures are to even a few degrees of change in the Earth's overall average temperature. Our climate's often unseeable changes affects everyone, regardless of one's place on Earth, identity, or status, as it is the quintessential representation of interrelationship and interdependence.[23]

Conclusion

The Spirit moves and creates new things. The Spirit is something that we cannot capture or contain. As I experienced the Holy Spirit as something which scared and frightened me in my youth, I was unable to talk about the Spirit in my life for a very long time—not until I reached seminary in my twenties. The Spirit long resided as a daunting concept in my life, and I even did everything I could to avoid it in my studies.

But as I entered seminary, the Spirit became a powerful way to speak about God. God exists in our world. We can often feel the presence of God in our lives. We can often experience God because God is always moving. Likewise, the Spirit is too. It is a form of vibration that fills our world.

There are the vibrations all around us. They are especially around us in worship, when our sanctuaries are filled with music. We are not sure how to explain it, but physicists state that creation and the entire universe is in movement or even in vibratory movement.

Nothing is static; there is a sense of vibration in all things. The Spirit as vibration has done many things, not only creating the world and shifting it in its entirety but also acting as a vehicle for forward change, moving us to act and reorient our own world.

---

23. Kim, *Colonialism, Han, and the Transformative Spirit*, 48.

Breathing is essential to vibrations, and in some ways, life is about having the right internal force. It is about connecting with others through the movement of vibrations and giving off the right vibes. Even the Pope asked the media, who do not pray, to at least "send him good vibrations."[24] Vibrations provide answers to how things work in this world.

The universe is full of vibrations, vibrations that should be in harmony with us. As we examine our life of high and low frequencies and the vibrations that exist in all intricate aspects of life, we recognize the Divine particle in all things, which also vibrate. As all things vibrate, we understand that the Spirit resides in all of us.

Spirit as vibration keeps us in motion and sustains our life. We need to allow the Spirit to vibrate through us so that we can become instruments for God.

---

24. See Pullella, "Pope Francis 'Prayer' Request."

CHAPTER 5

Spirit and Social Action

IF WE ARE TO be socially responsible people that create change in our world, then we need to be informed on what is happening around us. I believe that two of the greatest injustices that are happening today involve our relations with one another and our relations with our planet: racism and climate change. Racism is a powerful divider. It breaks communities and nations and starts war, forcing people to live within the confines of their skin color. It limits access and mobility, but most importantly, it limits the psyche of the marginalized.

Climate change will limit us in another devastating way, wiping away homes, cities, and whole countries. It will ravage life on Earth, causing lethal forest fires, earthquakes, hurricanes, and typhoons. Climate refugees will flee to certain regions of the world, fighting over resources and their allocation. World nations will quarrel with one another, their political powers feigning that they never saw it coming when they were warned of its arrival decades ago. Reflecting on these monumental issues, we may wonder what the relevance of the Spirit's role is in this. How can the Spirit help us overcome these problems and work towards a more just society? This chapter will explore these questions and work towards finding wholeness in healing.

Discrimination and the Spirit

Walls exist between the US and Mexico.[1] I have taken several seminary classes to the Mexico-US border through BorderLinks, an organization

---

1. Part of this section comes from a previously published blog. See Kim, "Walls That

that provides educational experiences to connect divided communities, raises awareness about the impacts of border and immigration policies, and inspires people to act for social reformation. My classes and I visited the metal wall that separates the United States from Mexico at Nogales, Mexico. The walls went up in 1994.

The North American Free Trade Agreement (NAFTA), established in 1994, was created with the intention to support world trade. It was strategized to strengthen Mexico's economic status in particular. However, this was a grave failure for our neighbors. The agreement backfired and made the economic environment despairingly worse for the people of Mexico. Wealthy American companies benefited from the Free Trade Agreement, as they were able to move their factories to Mexico where the labor was cheap and profits were higher. As the economy of Mexico suffered, more people without legal documentation made their way to the United States to seek work in hope of finding a better life for their families.

In 2006, the United States responded with the Secure Fence Act. As President George W. Bush signed the bill, he stated, "This bill will help protect the American people. This bill will make our borders more secure. It is an important step toward immigration reform."[2] The act included provisions for the construction of physical barriers—walls—and the use of technology to reinforce the walls.

This wall is under constant surveillance to prevent people from entering the US illegally. Ironically, it is a wall built from the metal scraps of the Gulf War. The border is militarized with patrols who mishandle migrants as prisoners of their war. It symbolizes the ugliness of American culture and politics: greed, hatred, pride, racism, and militarization, all expressions of a desire to protect and cultivate what you think is yours to solely keep for yourself.

Walls continue to go up along the border as many people in the United States are being fed the narrative that undocumented migrants will take away their jobs; these fears permeate the culture of fear in this country and only work to perpetuate the issue. As we ponder the roles these walls have played and the devastation their construction has caused, many people in the United States have begun to recognize that in continuing to build walls, we will only become further separated from the objectives they initially were founded on. They are a tangible allegory for the United States' own

---

Divide."

2. White House, "President Bush Signs Secure Fence Act."

staggering division among class, race, and politics. We need to break down the divisions. We need to break down the walls.

Another wall that I have encountered is that of the Korean peninsula. The border is called the DMZ, a "demilitarized zone." It was created in 1953, years after Korea was separated into two countries by the United States and the Soviet Union following World War II. This division continues to generate fear and hostility in both nations, and it is estimated today that over 10 million families are still separated by the DMZ.

I have visited the DMZ several times. One visit, I took two of my three children to see it. They are too young to remember the visit, but each time I visited the wall I was overcome with profound emotion. I could see it, hear it, feel it—the inexplicable devastation that this border signifies. The families separated, lives lost, friendships broken, and country torn in two.

At the border, there is a metal fence that divides the road traveling into the DMZ. Hundreds of letters, notes, flowers, and trinkets are left by families and strangers, woven into the fence to express pain and longing. So many Koreans dream of uniting with their separated families and hope that one day the wall can ultimately be dismantled. This brokenness, this wound, needs to be healed.

As we reflect on the walls of division around the world that divide people and ideologies, we recognize that if we want such walls to come down, we need to repair the broken ideologies and relationships that built them in the first place. We need to educate each other, young and old, on how to embrace the other, and help them lead dignified lives. Because in doing so, our lives will be enriched.

The hostility between the two Koreas needs to end as we work toward unity. Peace needs to be restored on this tiny peninsula, my homeland. Throughout this endeavor, our deep, and perhaps unrecognized fears of the other need to be abolished. Communication, dialogue, trust, and mutuality need to be restored, as only then will we find peace with the people we share the Earth with.

Climate Change

Human nature compels us to be with others; we are social creatures, creatures that have survived off of the congregation and support of our partners and our communities. As intelligent beings, this age has not only brought on the desire to survive but also the desire to find love. We long to connect with one another intimately and spiritually. The light within us can help us achieve this level of intimacy. The light attracts us to one another and keeps us connected. The light keeps us together and does not break the bonds between relationships. We need to love so that we can build solidarity with one another.

In September 2014, UN Secretary-General Ban Ki-moon held a climate summit with world leaders in New York City. While the event was significant, the work of such world leaders to address climate justice must not stop with prominent people or a climate summit. It is continual work within all countries, who need to dedicate themselves to lowering greenhouse gases, pursuing sustainability and environmental justice. Those in power must strive to develop an effective international plan to account for "out-of-state" pollution that crosses borders and contaminates our land, air, and water. It is clear: Lack of planning and action to save the environment will unquestionably end with devastation. Without the commitment and collaboration of each nation, each government, each community, and every individual, we will slip down the treacherous slope of complete environmental collapse.

Climate justice is a relatively new term in the realm of global social issues. The concept of climate justice is based on the idea that many of the changes in climate are contingent on the industrial and commercial activities of highly industrialized countries. They create negative environmental impacts on other countries that have had little to no participation in the production of these environmental impacts. These effects horribly manifest in human health and climate-displaced migration issues. They affect a wide range of human rights: the right to food, water, and sanitation, as well as the right to a safe environment. They inhibit and destroy agriculture and animal husbandry. Climate change is the most expansive example of human behavior's extraterritorial effects.

Climate justice also assumes that, while laws rarely bridge[3] national borders, countries can and should be held accountable for befouling the health and welfare of other countries. Therefore, in 1992, at the Rio Summit, the United Nations Framework Convention on Climate Change (UNFCCC) formed to address the issue of reducing greenhouse gas concentrations in the atmosphere. The Conference of the Parties (COP) was designated as the supreme governing body of the convention. This initiative

---

3. International affairs on the environment are under international organizations and international treaties.

Spirit and Social Action

has led to some positive action, and in 1997, the Kyoto Protocol, a binding instrument of the convention, was adopted. It established how much industrialized countries needed to reduce their CO_2 emissions.

At COP, 195 countries annually meet to share new statistics and information on greenhouse gas emissions, national policies, and optimal practices, as well as to negotiate how to prevent damage to ecological systems and protect agriculture from climate change. Discussions focus on adaptation, mitigation, climate finance, and transference of technology to support developing countries to combat practices that lead to climate change.

Coming from a wealthy nation, we are used to a certain kind of comfort and convenience in our lifestyles. As a result, we exploit the Earth's resources to make sure we live within a narrow comfort zone, where the typical agent of change is in the cultivation of material attainment. It seems that this issue is felt by many as a distant one. They may think, "If it is not my town that is flooding or my family who lost their home, then it doesn't concern me." Yet these are the people that tell their children that they are loved but continue to destroy their futures; the lives of their children's children. They are people only living for themselves in the present, ignorantly turning a blind eye to their own future lives. Us and the inevitable other will all have to pay the price eventually. This issue transcends all.

Nevertheless, adapting a lifestyle that lowers dependency on burned fuel (fossil or wood) and all other types of open air burning is a basic step that we can take to live a more conscious life. As we seek to identify other steps, we must recognize how developing technologies will be our greatest friend. They offer bountiful opportunity for research and development, resource conservation, renewable energy, cleaner practices—the list goes on.

God entrusts us with the stewardship of the Earth. As in the film *Noah*,[4] we understand that the flood depicted was punishment for bad stewardship of the land. This is an allegory that may start to resemble real life if climatic changes lead to events akin to Noah's great flood. God calls on us to care for the poor of the Earth and to live sustainably so all people might have life and have it in its whole fullness.

For many Christians, stewardship has become more about giving our money to the church than caring for God's creation. We have often misunderstood Genesis 1:28, "Be fruitful and increase in number; fill the earth and subdue it. Rule over the fish in the sea and the birds in the sky and

---

4. *Noah* is a biblical drama film directed by Darren Aronofsky and released in 2014.

over every living creature that moves on the ground," to legitimize human domination of the Earth and reinforce our own selfish agenda.

Christians have a long history of domination. In the name of evangelism, Christians have gone to the ends of the Earth to convert people to Christianity. European immigrants, many of them Christians, came to North and South America, conquered the indigenous peoples, participated in genocide, and dominated the continents. Many Christians today still live in this antiquated mentality of domination to subdue the Earth's resources and to ultimately exploit them.

Through the distortion of the Christian message, we Christians are major participants in distressing and damaging the Earth. When we consider the damage we inflict on the Earth and realize the depth of suffering this damage does to the created order—including the human family—we recognize that we have become the perpetrators of enormous *han* on the peoples of the Earth.

The global community of scientists argue that we cannot continue to live in this manner. Ice caps are melting, the sea level is rising, and the Earth is taking on irreversible destruction. Contrary to what some Christians may believe, climate change is real, and it affects everything. Climate change is one of *the* urgent issues of the world and of our time to remediate. Religious groups around the world have a responsibility to take action, to make the issue of climate change a leading priority, evaluating damaging practices and ceasing our abusive living.

WCC, Climate Change, and the Church

As institutions of authority, churches must change dramatically. The World Council of Churches (WCC) is a worldwide organization that strives for unity, to create a common witness, and to participate in Christian service. Its secretariat is based in Geneva, Switzerland. As a fellowship of churches, it is the most inclusive among the many organized expressions of the modern ecumenical movement, a movement whose goal is Christian unity. "The WCC brings together churches, denominations, and church fellowships in more than 110 countries and territories throughout the world, representing over 500 million Christians."[5] A unique group, the WCC reflects, acts, worships, and works together. It strives to challenge the church and to address pressing and pertinent issues.

5. WCC, "What Is the World Council of Churches?"

Spirit and Social Action

Dr. Guillermo Kerber, who was the WCC Programme Executive of Care for Creation and Climate Justice, believes that climate change is an ethical issue.[6] Those who are and will be suffering the most from the consequences of climate change have contributed the least to the causes. This is why it is a justice issue. For churches and other faith-based organizations, this struggle for human rights and justice is a component of their mission to serve human beings and all of creation.

As members of religious organizations, we believe that God created this beautiful world. God gave us everything we need for our survival and growth. People who are the weakest and most impoverished among us are the most affected by the hedonistic lifestyles in the First World, especially those of the United States. Due to our insatiable greed, we have gone down the path of self-destruction. While the issue has become more widespread in mainstream media and popular discourse, it is not a recent discovery. There were people aware of this problem in the 1960s who had an opinion about it:

> What have they done to the earth?
> What have they done to our fair sister?
> Ravaged and plundered and ripped her and bit her
> Stuck her with knives in the side of the dawn
> Jim Morrison, *When the Music's Over* (1968)

This reflects verses from Isaiah:

> The earth shall be utterly laid waste and utterly despoiled; for the LORD has spoken this word.
> The earth dries up and withers, the world languishes and withers; the heavens languish together with the earth.
> The earth lies polluted under its inhabitants; for they have transgressed laws, violated the statutes, broken the everlasting covenant.
> Therefore a curse devours the earth, and its inhabitants suffer for their guilt; therefore, the inhabitants of the earth dwindled, and few people are left. (Isa 24:3–6)

We must not forget the people who have been working for decades on remedying our dying Earth as well as the more recent ones. However, if humanity on a grander scale does not do its part, there may not be enough time to save the planet from destruction. Every church group needs to

---

6. Kerber, "Time to Convert."

recognize the urgency of this matter and take part in eco-justice. We are all called to be stewards of the Earth, and there is no time to act but now.

It is ever more important to recognize that we must carry the urgency of climate change into our religious outlooks on life. We cannot continue to ignore the topic of climate change in our faith, as Earth still suffers and burns in fever from overconsumption. We continue to fight for the freedom and dignity of all people, giving climate change and its correlated issues top priority. Fortunately, the WCC is making this a high priority, encouraging its member churches and all other churches in the world to unify and implement changes to heal the Earth and our environment.

Saving the planet is linked to economic issues. Without the urgency to tackle climate change, we cannot work on the economy. Climate change and the economy are intertwined; they exist as binaries. The assumption that investing in environmental policies will somehow weaken our economy or diminish our wealth is vastly misguided and false. It is completely feasible to strengthen both. And eventually expending on these issues will prove to create positive change through every social system and community. We should not rely on the efforts of the individual or esteemed groups but rather work with our neighbors to more effectively reinforce sustainable practices. There must be serious plans for theological engagement, advocacy, and action to work towards saving God's world.

As we reflect on racial and climate injustice, let us turn to the Spirit to find insight about how we can live better—how a global understanding of Spirit as light, wind, and vibration can move us to live justly.

Han of the Earth

Han is not limited to people. All of creation experiences pain and endures suffering. Creation suffers under the exploitative usage, pollution, and depletion of the Earth's resources. Toxins contaminate every space of modern society's land, killing off species and whole ecosystems. As humanity has advanced, our long-standing physical and social connections have been dismantled to be replaced by digital ones. Connection becomes more accessible but meaningful ones are rarified. Similarly, our once close connection to the Earth and its life has become far estranged.

The feminization of the Earth as "Mother Earth" may make it easier for humans to subjugate it. We tend to gender certain objects and concepts. Historically, the Earth has been viewed as mother by various cultures. Since the Earth is associated with the feminine, and the feminine is often regarded as weaker and subordinate, a framework has been subtly constructed that allows us to perceive the Earth to exist merely for us. When we allow that attitude to guide our actions, we damage the Earth.

Until recently, earthquakes were virtually unknown in Oklahoma. In the last few years, the state has experienced a rapid rise of earthquakes. Scientists are confident that the increasing emergence is human-made, caused by the fracking method,[7] which attempts to recover oil from the ground by forming deep wells and disposing polluted water into holes. Several of these earthquakes were at 3.0 or greater on the Richter scale, meaning that humans (in addition to seismic instruments) felt them. The Earth is crying out from pain and the burden of its *han*.

We have bought into the capitalist-driven delusion that nothing will run out. Dr. Jeffrey Sachs, director of the Earth Institute,[8] reminds us that we cannot continue to believe the Earth is a "supermarket." Such a view wrongly teaches us to turn a blind eye to the resource depletion we contribute to and to continue living as if there are no limits.

There are still many people that refuse to believe that this issue exists. There is perhaps no better parable of this than the recent film *Noah* (2014), where the reason for the Creator's reset on creation is because humans have exhausted all the natural resources.

We need to understand that we cannot continue to live the way the elite have come to accept as their right because they have the money to do so. Liberation theology tells us we need to turn that ethic on its head. We need to live with a "preferential option for the poor." That is, we need to emphasize the physical welfare of the poor and powerless, as this will in turn enrich our lives through giving meaning to our actions.

Thus the environment presents itself as the new frontier in which we need to fight for social justice. If we understand that our actions will degrade our lives and affect generations to come, will we change our ways? Part of the problem is that we do not even recognize the deep impact of many of these changes.

For example, after the extermination of the wolf population in Yellowstone National Park, the environment deteriorated due to an increase in the elk. They overgrazed the river bank grass and depleted the population of healthy trees by stripping them of their bark and eroding them.

---

7. Zukowski, "5.0 Earthquake Hits Oklahoma."
8. Kim, "Care for the Whole Creation."

The absence of wolves also generated the increase of the coyote population, inducing the depletion of the pronghorn antelope. In 1995, wolves were reintroduced into Yellowstone and the effect was dramatic. The elk population dropped and the ecosystem along rivers and streams recovered. Similarly, the coyote population dropped with a concomitant increase in beaver dams in the park.[9]

When I look around, it is hard not to see how ignorantly we live our lives. I say this as someone who also has tendencies to turn away from issues I thought did not directly involve me. It stems from this notion that if we are not privy to immediate ramifications, then we have no responsibility for any of the consequences of it. This perspective, in combination with our individualism and greed, allows us to deny the damage we do to creation. The longer we stay in denial, the closer we inch to our own destruction. The healing of Earth's *han* can only begin if we begin to live a life of eco-sufficiency and eco-justice. For the actions we take tomorrow, are already too late.

Culture, Differences, and the Spirit

The world we are living in is globalized. We are the most diverse we have ever been and more aware than ever of those who differ from us: those who live in the landscapes of the "exotic," those who populate powerful nations, those who inhabit regions in secluded worlds, and perhaps even those who grow up right next to us. This new age we enter is wondrously connected, encouraging us to make neighbors with those we once thought were mere strangers.

As we reflect on the Spirit as light, wind, breath, and vibration, it expands our explorations of the Spirit to understand that the concept of Spirit exists in other religions, cultures, and societies. Drawing from my previous work on the Spirit,[10] it is crucial that we continue to reimagine the Spirit in the biblical terms of light, wind, breath, and vibration as well as explore other ways of understanding the Spirit that are aligned with the Bible.

Our new world of inter-reliance has augmented our growth as a society, but it has also brought on new responsibilities in order for us to live in greater understanding and harmony. As time goes on, international travel

---

9. Peglar, "1995 Reintroduction of Wolves in Yellowstone."
10. For more of my work on the Spirit, see Kim, *Holy Spirit, Chi, and the Other*.

will become even more accessible and efficient, bringing foreign faces into new lands.

Inevitably, the more diverse homogenous communities become, the greater the chance of initial prejudice. Being a foreigner in any land engenders a different kind of treatment, and unfortunately for some, this means inferior treatment. Therefore, the more cultures collide, the greater our obligation to find common ground.

One such commonality may be an understanding of the Spirit,[11] which is present in many cultures; therefore, it is important to address the question of whether there is one Spirit or many. Christianity generally maintains that it presents the true Spirit and that all the other spirits found around the world are lesser or evil, but the Spirit that is light, wind, and vibration that we find in Christianity is the same Spirit that exists everywhere. Experiences and images of this Spirit occur in our natural world and are not exclusive to Christians. If this is so, what are the implications? And how are we to process such understandings in light of a shrinking world, where we are living and interacting with people from all walks of life, cultures, and faith traditions?

An open-ended notion of Spirit[12] will help us work toward finding shared ground between different cultures. The Spirit of light, wind, and vibration that is experienced by non-Christians, foreigners, immigrants, and all others will surely change our ways of thinking, acting, and interacting with our neighbors, friends, and foreigners.

Hybridity and Mixing of Cultures

When we talk about those who migrate to the United States, such migrants become cultural "hybrids." You may know Asian Americans who are hybrids, as they have amalgamated their Asian background with the surrounding Euro-American culture and created a new Asian American culture. This occurs in language as well, as new mixed vocabularies emerge in casual speech.

---

11. Spirit, *chi, qi*—or some other name—may mean spirit, but it may not be a part of a major world religion. Two examples are the notion of spirit in yoga and in the martial art, tai chi. Yoga is a practical part of both Hindu and Buddhist variations, but it is practiced independently as part of the Indian culture by millions, beginning in the early nineteenth century.

12. Even one where spirit may not include the notion of breath.

For example, Korean Americans often speak "Kon-glish," which is the combination of Korean and English fused into a synthesized dialect. This entails expressing English words with a Korean accent so it feels as though we are speaking Korean. As a daughter of Korean immigrant parents, I was greatly impacted by the use of language and the adaptation technique of hybridity.

As a result, looking back, my childhood was full of embarrassing moments, the majority of which are experiences of demeaning failures of trying to fit into white culture. I could not speak proper English when I first immigrated at age five, but from age nine I rapidly acculturated to Canada. However, as my parents spoke mostly Korean, both at work and at home, their acculturation was significantly slower, and the barriers of communication between us started to form. This was not only limited to language—though this was a large part of the issue—but also had to do with cultural clashes. No child wants to be a misfit, but that is exactly how I felt all the time.

We survived by speaking "Kon-glish" to each other, which was commonly comprehended by other Korean-Canadian immigrants. We swiftly moved from one language to another, often without even realizing it, combining words together to make a brand new "Kon-glish" word. This new lexicon created a common vocabulary that every Korean American would understand. For instance, when cellphones became more popular, we started to refer to them as *haen-deu-pon*, a Korean pronunciation of handphone. When new words emerged, they were hybrids, just as Yiddish is a hybrid of German and Hebrew. As such, hybridization occurred whether we were conscious of it or not.

Coming back to the discussion of the Holy Spirit, it is important to recognize the globalization of theology and Christianity. As Christianity expands, it, too, needs to recognize its own limitations of being a theology limited to particular European languages, such as English, French, German, Spanish, Dutch, Latin, Greek, and Russian.[13] If there is to be any hope of Christianity becoming more global and accepting of all peoples, it is necessary to liberate Christian concepts as malleable, especially in dialogues on the Holy Spirit. It is becoming ever more crucial to recognize *chi*, African spiritualities, South American shamanist practices, Native American

---

13. In this regard, Christianity works on the notion of spiritual inspiration of translated Scripture, making them as sacred as the original Hebrew and Greek.

spiritualities, and other spiritual practices and concepts in order to recognize the richness of the work and movement of the Spirit.

In this regard, Christianity believes in the spiritual inspiration of translated Scripture, rendering various translated Scriptures as sacred as the original Hebrew and Greek Scriptures. Christianity has the advantage of beginning with a dual language heritage, giving it an advantage over Islam, which is far more closed than Christianity in regards to language and the authority of a single linguistic source.

My mother had strong opinions about Christianity. One of them was her love for Christianity and dislike of other religions, as she believed they were all wrong. She tried to instill in me a fear of others, different cultures, and particularly those who were not Christians. She claimed that other forms of spirituality were false and that they would lead me down the wrong path. As a young adolescent, I had endless unanswered questions and experienced great discomfort. However, the more I study and engage with different spiritualities and gain an informed understanding of how different cultures view the Spirit, the more I come to realize and accept the global transcendence of the Spirit itself.

People are afraid of the unknown and often demonize others who have different beliefs and customs. This can be seen in the way North Americans and Europeans have demonized Islam because of what Islamic terrorists have done. However, protecting some idea of orthodoxy may not be important to a God who says, "I WILL BE WHO I WILL BE" (Exod 3:14). Eurocentric Christianity is not as governing or as significant as it once was. Christianity is becoming less relevant to white Europeans and white Americans as it moves to the global South and the dominant Christian languages become Spanish, Bantu, and Afro-Semitic dialects. As Christianity moves southward, we need to recognize the power of spiritualities that have existed in these cultures for thousands of years. As we recognize the breadth and scope of the Holy Spirit experienced by people around the world, we recognize the opportunity to open and redefine the Spirit of our own Christian faith.

New Pneumatology

While the unification of distinct cultures has generally followed a strict narrative, whereby the dominant culture subjugates, oppresses, or appropriates the culture of the minority culture, contemporary times are slowly rerouting that historical process. Today, we have matured from many of these ill practices and have created new alliances and forms of support. Entering this landscape of constant interaction and cultivating interdependence brings on a responsibility to communicate better. As people move out of their culture of origin, many will face stereotypes and racism when they arrive in a new land. Therefore, as cultures interact, it is important to discover the things we have in common or a means of positive interaction to enrich one another.

One such potential commonality is an understanding of the Spirit, which is present in many cultures, including Christianity; therefore, it is important to ask whether there is one Spirit or many. Christianity has often implied that it possesses the true Spirit and that all the other spirits found in other scriptures and theologies around the world are lesser or evil. An open-ended notion of Spirit may work towards finding common ground with people from different cultures.

Asian *Chi*

Culture defines us; it is one of the most formative and prescribed forms of personal and learned identity, informing our thought processes and shaping our beliefs on how to live and co-exist across cultures. Culture carves out a principled way for us to live, and in particular, it dictates how that way of life will offer reverence for our predecessors. It inextricably connects us to our past and pushes us to pass down the same patterns of behavior to younger generations. It is part of what makes us a necessary tile-piece in the mosaic of a community—something greater—but also part of what makes us individuals. I invite you to explore with me how Asian culture can shape our understanding of Spirit through the lens of *chi*.

Just as *chi* is ambiguous, the biblical words for Holy Spirit—*ruach* in the Old Testament and *pneuma* in the New Testament—are also ambiguous: wind symbolizes a powerful force in nature and breath symbolizes the power of life in living things. Without *chi*, life does not exist, and similarly, if there is no Spirit, nothing can live. So it seems that there is a significant overlap between the Western-Christian notion of Spirit and the Asian understanding of *chi*. And in an increasingly multireligious, multilingual, and multicultural world, recognizing the differences and similarities among people, cultures, and religions is essential. Religions in different parts of the world do not display many spirits; rather, in them we find various names for the Spirit. So it is entirely appropriate for a book on the Holy Spirit of the Christian tradition to begin with an investigation of *chi*.

Just as racism is a social sickness, individuals who experience spiritual brokenness may also experience physical ailment. An understanding of the association of *chi* with the Holy Spirit or identification of *chi* as the Holy Spirit enables us to learn that *chi* is divine and is the true healer of bodies. *Chi* has been and is continually being used in healing. Chinese emperors, philosophers, and physicians have understood healing with the movement of *chi* in the body. Most believed that illnesses occurred when one's *chi* was blocked and therefore it was important to redirect the *chi* to flow within the body. In traditional Korean practice, these beliefs are still held. Hence, the understanding of *chi* is fundamental to healing oneself.

Han blocks the flow of *chi*. *Han* stops the Spirit from being the light, wind, and vibration of the world. *Han* has devastating effects in us and prevents us from being the light of the Spirit from within us. Thus *han* needs to be removed to enable a freer flow of *chi*. A good flow of *chi* means a healthier body and mind.

Global Spirit

In our contemporary world, the idea of individuals from divergent cultures, socioeconomic classes, and religions living together is becoming more widely accepted and more necessary. It creates a window of opportunity for different religions and schools of thought to marry into new perspectives and create a more meaningful Christianity for today.

In this context, it is important to recognize the differences and the similarities among cultures and religions. This world is suffused with the Spirit, and the Spirit needs to be recognized by people of all cultures. Besides *ruach*, *pneuma*, and *chi*, there are other terminologies in various cultures that capture this idea of Spirit/breath and God. As we examine the religions found in different parts of the world, we will find that there are not many spirits; rather, we find various names for one Spirit. The Spirit that is light, wind, and vibration is also present in different parts of the world. God's Spirit is so powerful that, Pentecost-like, it breaks down the language walls that human beings have built between themselves. Spirit as vibration will go through barriers that people have set up against one another and tear down those walls. Spirit as light will penetrate darkness to bring light into the world, and the Spirit as wind will breathe new life into dry bones. This is a global Spirit that knows no boundaries.

God's Spirit is the divine energy that hovers over the Earth as it vibrates and permeates creation. It is in deep meditation that we can unite with God through the energy and resonance throughout the Earth. This was written in the biblical creation narratives in Genesis 1 and 2. As Christian theology works toward a worldwide notion of the Spirit, it is important to expand its concepts beyond only the economic Trinitarian notions of the Spirit. When we think of the concept of a missional church, we recognize that we do not "go there," but rather that God is already there. We understand that God has always already been working in other cultures. God is present in the world. This should be the understanding of a missional church.

The Asian understanding of *chi* has notable implications for a global pneumatology. It embodies the understanding of Spirit as light, wind, and vibration as it exists in the physical world and is embodied in us. We experience the Spirit in these different manifestations. Furthermore, as people experience discrimination, sexism, racism, and otherness, *chi*, in combination with the Holy Spirit, gives them a connection to their past as it is embedded in their cultural being and helps them move forward into the future. It is part of the psyche, incorporating this common yet powerful concept.

Dualism

Christianity has emphasized the Greco-Roman dichotomy between body and spirit. The spirit was good and the body was evil. All that had to do with the body was viewed as negative, thus there was a separation between the body and spirit. This dualistic understanding is detrimental today, as it reinforces an asceticism based on the sinfulness of the body.

A pneumatology of Spirit-*chi* will provide a new understanding of the Spirit to unite body and spirit with fewer pejorative connotations. Such understandings will work toward diminishing harmful interpretations of the dichotomy between body and spirit as well as between men and women. A liberation from dualism will allow people to experience harmony. For our contemporary world to thrive, it is becoming increasingly necessary to adopt and share a more harmonious understanding of the Spirit.

Saint Paul distinguished between the Holy Spirit and "my spirit" in Romans. It is Paul's spirit that preaches the gospel of God's Son (Rom 1:9).

It is Paul's own spirit that is challenged, which may or may not be joined with the Holy Spirit. Jesus himself states in the Beatitudes that a person's spirit may be weak ("Blessed are the poor in spirit" [Matt 5:3]). Meister Eckhart speaks of losing one's own spirit and joining with the Spirit of God. The West largely recognizes a separation of human and divine Spirit due to the influence of dualism. This perception may tend to further separate us from Spirit and each other. Rather than understanding that God is with us, in us, and among us, we have made the Spirit a secondary person of the Trinity who is not involved in our lives.

We want to be able to communicate with each other. We often try, but in some cases our limited vocabulary may prevent us from doing so successfully. If we do not maintain an open mind, our thoughts and understandings will eventually come to restrict us.

The same thing happens in Christian theology. We are often bound to the limitations imposed upon us by white, Eurocentric theology. We need to free ourselves from these limitations. We need to go beyond our preconceived ideas and thought patterns—and even beyond our limiting English language—to seek other vocabularies that can help us articulate something so vast, so mysterious, and so infinite as the Spirit God. Therefore, it seems necessary to theological survival to search the world for words and expressions to articulate God, such as Spirit-*chi*. It not only draws on the global context of pneumatology but also the biblical understanding of the Spirit as light, wind, breath, and vibration.

Even Korean Christians Ignore *Chi*

Chi is virtually unknown among Christians of European, African, and South American heritage. But it might be surprising to learn that *chi* is often ignored by Korean Christians, too. The majority resist using their own heritage, deferring to the dominant, Eurocentric understanding. Korean Christians were initially taught by missionaries to remove, revoke, and disengage any non-Christian religious practices and teachings, and this meant that anything non-European was often considered non-Christian. Korean Christians neither welcomed any hybridity creeping into their religion nor any notion of syncretism flowing into their newfound Christian practices. White missionaries taught Korean converts to rid themselves of any remnants of Shamanism, Confucianism, or Buddhism after their conversions. Korean Christians abided faithfully—or at least that is what they thought.

Reimagining Spirit

We know that every religion is influenced by other religions and practices. Even with the careful removal of non-Christian teachings and practices within Korean Christianity, we see remnants of Shamanism, Confucianism, and Buddhism remain. This is evident in their way of worship, prayer, and fellowship.

Confucianism is rigid when it comes to gender roles. It commonly limits the interaction of men and women. This is evidenced within Korean American Christian congregations. Many churches will serve a meal after Sunday worship. However, among the Korean American Christians, tables are designated to be seated with either men or with women. Men and women also worship separately, and seldom do they mix. This gender separation occurs in various forms of fellowships.

So my challenge to Euro-Christians, Asian Christians—all Christians!—is to look to the concept of *chi* to fill out our understanding of the Holy Spirit. In the early pictorial language of *chi*, the Chinese used a pictogram, a pictorial image symbolizing a word or phrase, of a bowl of rice with steam rising.

People in most of Asia, particularly in East Asia, live on rice. Rice truly is life. It is the foundation of every meal, sustaining our forebears with its pervasive accessibility and starchy nutrient. It is a necessary staple in our lives. During the Korean War, when my grandmother was escaping with her young children at the peak of crisis, she only had minutes to prepare her kids before she fled south. In that moment, she packed a small pouch of rice, which she managed to carry in her pants pocket. She was able to use that rice to cook meals on the road for her seven small children. That bag of rice was the only thing she managed to take from home.

To Koreans, the spirit of life is *chi*. The Hebrews used the term *ruach*; the New Testament writers used *pneuma*; and the German theologians of the eighteenth and nineteenth centuries used *Geist*, a word meaning a combination of spirit and mind. *Chi* is as engrossed in a culture as any of these other terms, but that does not make it inaccessible to non-Asians. To the contrary, cross-pollinating this term with *ruach, pneuma,* and *Geist* will only make our understanding of God's Spirit fuller and richer.

In the West, we have made Spirit a philosophical notion to be contemplated abstractly but not lived with and truly understood. The early Pentecostal experience of the church and its people has been long forgotten, and many of the dull church practices have now become standard practice. The awe and fear of the Spirit that the Hebrew people experienced is long forgotten, and now many of us treat it not as a living Spirit but rather as a concept that is lost in the traditions of the church. It has become more of a philosophical idea that is ruminated on by intellectuals and not a life-giving Spirit, felt and experienced by all in their day-to-day lives. As Asians are often conscious of *chi* and Spirit in everyday life and in daily existence, it is past time for more church members to now do likewise.

The long philosophical tradition of the Holy Spirit has caused it to become a *thing* rather than a *being*. This makes it a part of the godhead with no agenda of its own. We have made it an object to discuss and debate but not something that we live by or live through. And that's where *chi* can complement and correct our usual understanding of Spirit since *chi* is a dynamic life-force. Spirit-*chi* is a living energy, not merely the third paragraph of the Nicene Creed.

We need to be more conscious of the living, indwelling presence of Spirit in our midst and in our lives and of how its connection to God is an asset. We need to build a language for the Spirit as it opens the door for us and strengthens our understanding of the mysterious God. We are to be creative and dynamic when we try to understand the mysterious power of God. As we recognize the power of *chi* flowing in our bodies and in our lives, we can share it with others to make the world a better, more peaceful place to live.

The Spirit of God seems to have become an object to be studied rather than a divine being. The church continues to debate the existence and definition of the Spirit rather than allowing the Spirit to become and be who she is. Just as YHWH stated in the burning bush, "I will be who I will be." People get wrapped up in orthodoxy rather than good practice (orthopraxy), and as a result, the Spirit becomes confined, choking the freedom that it needs to flourish.

We have inherited a very philosophical understanding of the Holy Spirit, one that diverges from reality and the materiality of our flawed human lives. It makes it difficult to imagine the Spirit in any different way. Christianity has been so entrenched in the Western, white, Eurocentric mindset that it has silenced all other voices around the globe. Furthermore, the Spirit has been too often ignored in many mainline denominations. It has been relegated to a junior position in the Trinity rather than its deserving position as an important, full-fledged member. It may prove difficult to diverge from this common status, but I hope through my teaching and writing that this convention is disrupted and revolutionized.

Steps to Release *Han*

It may be said that one of the great pursuits of a Christian life is to attain "wholeness" as well as "holiness." To achieve wholeness, as a gift of the Spirit and a gift of grace, there needs to be healing in the face of injustice, abuse, and violence. Wholeness can be achieved by redirecting our existing *han* to work proactively, rendering our surroundings as a place that is more just for all.

One of the great injustices of many modern societies is the inequitable distribution of wealth. Buttressed on a system that encourages the socially advantaged to grow their wealth grossly un-proportioned to the poor while remaining on top, the gap between economic positions widens to only further subjugate the unprivileged. While this issue is deeply embedded in most major global societies, we need to start small and fight for domestic causes that will ultimately feed into a larger battle.

Another step is to eliminate the material clutter in our individual and national lives and to recognize just how great our overconsumption is. It is not us that have to face the grim repercussions of our wasteful lifestyles but those who have had no involvement at all. We must rightfully and firmly introduce new ways of living, sharing what we have, and supporting those in need. In capitalist societies like America, you don't have to look far to see that the majority of the wealthy are less inclined to apportion their resources for the benefit of the country as a whole; they are more inclined to wield their personal wealth towards gaining a greater asset, power. With the power that comes from money, they are able to facilitate their own agendas; whether it may be "charitable," for the common good, or self-interested.

The values of acquisitiveness create *han* for those who have nothing, and while it is more through ignorance than through malice, it is *han* nonetheless. If we are serious about saving our planet, life, and humankind, then we must understand nature's *han*. Trees, water, air, and soil have been destroyed by human greed, graft, and ignorance. Human actions that contradict the will of nature produce *han*, making nature plea under the weight of this oppression; whether it is organic life or the elements themselves, there is will and thus there is *han*.

The Bible has taught this idea of the *han* within all of creation (Rom 8:19–23), yet we have not taken it seriously. We have ignored the *han*-ridden cry of nature and animals that have been the subject of our ill-intended actions in the form of ecological downfall and natural or produced disasters. It is time for humanity to repent for its anthropocentric sin against nature and animals. In order to achieve a holistic vision of the common good, the human race must move resolutely to dissolve the *han* of animals and nature.[14]

We are dependent on one another and we always have been. When we realize that our neighbor's *han* is our *han* and that theirs is ours, we enter a new dimension of humanity, one that is compassionate and emotionally intelligent. We know little of our *han* unless we know the *han* of others. Once we finally realize our indivisible interconnectedness, everyone, including the oppressors, can cooperate to dissolve the *han* of the oppressed. Our own and our children's and grandchildren's survival and happiness—even our very relationships with God—depend on our faithful actions now.[15]

The first step should always be to search your own traditions. Everyone, not just the Koreans, Navajos, and Catholics, have liturgies of spiritual peace. But if no traditional method presents itself, consider these steps in how we can spiritually save ourselves by eliminating our *han*:

A first step is to recognize that *han* exists in our lives. Many people do not want to confront it or fail to understand the pain in their hearts that comes from unjust suffering. However, one must recognize this deep pain, accept it, and take the necessary measures to learn from it and heal.

This recognition needs to include a spiritual and soulful understanding. It involves turning to the Spirit. The Spirit as light helps us recognize that we are all a light in the world and therefore become a beacon to others. The Spirit moves us and helps us become more cognizant beings, encouraging us to recognize the debilitating and hurtful power that *han* can have in one's life. Turning to the Spirit helps us acknowledge the need for help—help that can enable us to eliminate the *han* from our lives and from the Earth.

The second step is to allow ourselves to be open to the Spirit's movement within us. We need to be fully aware of our hearts, guarding them from the effects of *han* and the dangers of harboring *han* within. The Spirit convinces our hearts of the damaging pain of *han*. The Spirit-*chi* should be embodied. Embodied Spirit-*chi* can open us up to ultimate freedom, allowing us to change ourselves and the world for the better. Without *chi*, we are unable to make these positive changes in our lives.

We must allow the Spirit to take over our bodies and our lives. We need to be willing to be overcome with Spirit-*chi*. *Chi* is energy, life-giving,

---

14. Park, *Wounded Heart of God*, 44.
15. Kim, *Colonialism, Han, and the Transformative Spirit*, 54.

and breath. All these things are necessary to live a healthy, fulfilled life. With *han* controlling us, we cannot live in full health and realized spirituality. We need to surrender to the Spirit. In doing so, we allow the rhythm of the vibrations from the Spirit to reside within us and shine through us.

The last step is to allow the Spirit to make good vibrations in our heart, soul, and body. The entire world is full of vibrations. There are harmonies and dissonances, quarrels between lovers, and wars between nations. These create tensions and therefore movements—vibrations. We need to allow the Spirit to make vibrations into our lives and bring healing into our hearts. *Han* is debilitating, so we need good vibrations to fill our bodies and our souls. When we fill our bodies and souls with the dynamic vibrations and rhythms of the Spirit, the *han* is alleviated in our lives. In life-giving ways, we must be open to the movements of the Spirit in our bodies, our lives, and on the Earth.

The harmonies within us will then send out further vibrations that will in turn make this world a better place to live. This initiates a positive cycle of goodness that circulates from us to the greater environment. The damage that *han* can create in our lives is replaced as we release it through the help of the Spirit. When we are truly open, the power of the Spirit can release and ultimately heal our *han*. Being open to the vibrations of Spirit and allowing the Spirit to take over will eliminate our *han* and allow us to grow into the best versions of ourselves.

Spirit Heals *Han*

While I was in the Master of Divinity program, I spent many solitary hours in the Knox College chapel. It is an old stone chapel with large sweeping arches and a golden, stained glass window at the front. It is large, positioned on the south side of Knox College, with a wide middle aisle, stone floors, and wooden pews. It has become a favorite venue for weddings, and all summer long, you will see couples get married in the historic walls of the building. I have so many beautiful memories of this chapel, and one of my closest friends married there, where I was one of her bridesmaids. I can still remember when the seminary organist played hymns on the old pipe organ, the floor beneath my feet, the bench I sat on, and my whole body were vibrating.

Though the chapel remains a place of fond memories to me, it is also a place that has held onto the pains and pleading prayers of its residents.

There were many times when I was in school that my pain and *han* were too much, and I sought refuge in the chapel. I talked to God and cried, asking for a change, some form of release from my sufferings. And after four years of my troubled cries and prayers, one day I felt a cathartic release. It was an enormous detachment of all the emotional burdens I felt weighing down on me as I felt the movement of the Spirit within me. The Spirit came and brought peace to my heart. It stirred new life into my broken being. It was in that moment that I came to the realization of how the Spirit releases our *han* and heals our hearts.

The Spirit will ultimately release *han* and bring healing to our lives. The Spirit as *chi*, discussed in chapter 1, can fill us and bring the rightful Spirit flow back into our bodies, empowering and helping us to live healthy lives. It will comfort us and bring wholeness when we are at our most broken.

Healing occurs in the physical, psychological, and spiritual realms within us. *Han* can damage parts of us, and it is the Spirit that can heal all those damaged areas in our lives. It is not just human beings that can be healed. All of God's creation can be healed. As the power of the Spirit as wind, vibration, and light flows freely on the Earth, it can bring healing to the damage caused by the greed, exploitation, and consumerism that we undertake and that surrounds us. The Spirit can begin to heal the damage to the Earth as it releases the harmful effects of *han*. Both humanity and the Earth can be healed by the movement of the Spirit.

The wounds caused by *han* are boundlessly deep. The only way that healing can fully take place is through the power of the Spirit. This healing can allow us to move forward to a brighter future. The light within will bring tremendous joy to the surface of our lives that remains plunged below when *han* is overbearing.

This healing can only come through the deepest understanding of the Spirit as the giver of grace and mercy. Grace and mercy are needed to bring healing into our lives. The Spirit as light and vibration warms our hearts and souls that have been damaged and brings wholeness to them. The vibrations and movements of the Spirit can bring forth new life in us and in all of creation. We need to be open to the energy, movement, and life-giving power of the Spirit to bring us to wholeness.

We live in a world fragmented by our sinful ways of living. Despite this brokenness, God cares for all of creation. All people are children of God, and all are beloved by God. God invites us to remember this love and to unify in building God's reign. Healing of the Earth is required for this to occur.

Being open to the Spirit's power and allowing it to work within us and in all of creation will miraculously transform our *han*, broken relationships, sinful systems, and destructive ways of living. The Spirit that hovers over all the Earth can bring the ultimate healing to both the Earth and its inhabitants.

Conclusion

Spirit's World

THE WORLD IS FILLED with the Spirit. Everywhere you look, the presence of the Spirit is felt. As we travel around the world, we recognize and witness the work of the Spirit in our churches, our communities, and our families. The Spirit both lives in the world and works in our lives. The presence of the Spirit is undeniable. The Spirit is light, wind, and vibration; it is all around us and in us.

As we see the work of the Spirit around the globe, one question in particular arises. Does the Spirit belong solely to Christianity? If the Spirit is light, wind, and vibration, does it exist outside the Christian church, and can it be present in the life of other faith traditions? It is with this question that we seek to gain a better understanding of the Holy Spirit and the Spirit within us. In turn, this informs our global understanding that the Holy Spirit is the Christian vision of a universal human perception. The Spirit is God, and no one community can hold or possess it. It is free and able to move as it wishes in the world. The gift of life and the struggle for the equality of life are sustained by the Spirit's power, and this cannot be simply contained within the Christian church or tradition.

The Spirit proceeds from the whole world and manifests itself in nature.[1] While Christians tend to understand the Spirit in relation to the Trinity, it is helpful to consider the ways in which other faiths see it in relation to the body. We need to be aware of this presence and make room for its participation, allowing it to permeate our lives and to move and work within us. Whenever we welcome and embrace the Spirit within our lives,

1. Hodgson, *Christian Faith*, 140.

we draw nearer to God. God is in all things because all things are in God. God is ubiquitous: God is wherever creation is.[2] God is all around us. The Spirit empowers us and possesses us to act, taking care of each other and of creation. It begs us to deepen our knowledge of God and challenges us to search the world for more nuanced ways of speaking and interacting with the divine.

It is important that we work to free the Spirit so that we do not restrain the movement and work of the Spirit through our limited understanding. To do so, we must to recognize the freedom of the Spirit. One cannot say that the Spirit only belongs to Christians—the Spirit moves around the whole globe and is present in all places. One might find that people of different faiths also experience and articulate the Spirit in their lives. The Spirit is freely moving and cannot be contained, and Christianity surely cannot commandeer it based on how they have experienced God. In Judeo-Christian scripture, God says "I AM WHO I AM" (Exod 3:14), which demonstrates that the movement of God is not constrained by what human beings dictate.

Under European colonization, Christianity has tried to monopolize the Divine Spirit for far too long. Christianity has instructed and claimed that only Christianity possesses the Spirit, arguing that all other "spirits" or experiences of the "spirit" are false. As Christianity colonized different parts of the world, it spread its theologies of God and the Spirit, overcoming Islam, Hindu religions, and Buddhism. Christianity sought to present itself as the superior religion that understood and maintained control of the Divine Spirit. Supposedly only Christianity could grasp divine understanding and comprehension of the Spirit. According to that worldview, one would have to follow Christianity to experience the Divine Spirit and truly understand it. This history of monopolization of the Spirit must be reexamined, reconsidered, and challenged.

When Christianity plays an imperial role, it has the tendency to view itself as a belief system superior to oral cultures. As a result, the primordial stranger becomes the Other—a stranger unlike us and less worthy than we are. However, beautiful things are bound to happen when we come to recognize the stranger among us. We understand that this Spirit cannot be constrained and contained within Christianity. The Spirit moves freely as a manifestation of a God who says "I AM WHO I AM" (Exod 3:14). We

---

2. McFague, "Dearest Freshness Deep Down Things," 117.

cannot safeguard the Spirit within Christianity and present it to the world as something exclusively for Christians to encounter.

When the American astronaut Scott Kelly posted pictures on his Twitter account of the Earth, it became clear to me the scale of humanity within the grandiosity of the Earth. Clearly, Christians are not the center of the universe. Christians cannot hold onto something that "hovers over the surface of the water" (Gen 1:2) and proclaims "I WILL BE WHAT I WILL BE" (Exod 3:14). Given that the Spirit is boundless, it is naïve for Christians to claim that only our Spirit is holy. In so many ways, the Spirit opens rather than closes the door for us to be in conversation with other world religions. Thus the presence of the Spirit creates an "open space," wherein we encounter the Other in his or her full dignity and uniqueness.

The Christian doctrine of the Spirit has the potential to open space for interfaith dialogue. As the Spirit moves in our lives and gives us breath, life, and sustenance, we become open to various movements of the Spirit in all places, traditions, cultures, and religions. This is the movement of the Spirit that no single person, doctrine, or church can control.

Living in a dynamic time, when the world is technologically advancing and quickly diversifying, is an exciting new prospect; a new world where varied peoples come together as neighbors and form new cultures. However, as we enter such a world of interdependence, we must be able to communicate cross-culturally in order to create harmony. Therefore, as cultures collide with one another, it is important to find common ground.

Life Isn't Fair

Generally, good people will say that they hope for a world where all lives are valued fairly and where those who do bad are punished accordingly. We want to see the innocent happy and liberated and the corrupt penalized and incarcerated. But we know that this idealistic fantasy is far from reality.

As I raise my three children, I often notice that all three do not receive the same treatment. I know I am the harshest towards my oldest son when he does something wrong. I believe that if he succeeds or does well, then there will be a trickle-down effect, and the other two siblings will also succeed. Furthermore, by the time the youngest gets in trouble for the same thing, I am too exhausted to discipline him. So one might say that he gets away with everything. Even the older two kids notice it, and they frequently remark, "Mom, you don't punish him enough."

But equal uniform treatment is just not possible when dealing with people, particularly teenagers. Inevitably, I fall into the trap of behaving differently towards each child, treating them as I believe they need to be treated in the moment, with attention to their individual needs. It has both positive and negative impacts, but as parents, we must use our best judgment and keep our children as the ultimate priority.

As we go through life, it becomes clear that the nicest people do not always win. Sometimes the worthy get the raw end of the deal, and their less deserving counterparts reap benefits.

In certain ways, when we think about grace, it is the same thing. Grace is not about getting what we deserve or about getting just punishment. Instead, grace is an opportunity for us to escape the consequential sufferings for our actions. And for many people, this is upsetting.

We want people to get what they deserve. But God is not like that. The beauty of God is revealed to us in God's Spirit, which manifests as grace toward all people.

God's Spirit and Grace

The Holy Spirit is the gift to the world. It is grace to us. God's grace is transformative as it changes and makes us anew. The Spirit is grace that changes us and changes the world. We are to build the kin-dom of God through the power of the Holy Spirit as grace.

For Augustine, the Holy Spirit is the uncreated grace (*gratia increata*). Thus, grace and justification are understood as the effects of the Holy Spirit.[3] Grace is participation in the Divine or, in other words, grace is divine nature. It is given to us and resides in us. Grace is about being set free. The Spirit frees us from the burden of trying to prove ourselves worthy, good, and desirable. The Spirit sets us free to be carefree and to be ourselves. It frees us to move as the wind. This will allow the Spirit to move within us and fill us so that the Spirit can move us.

We emphasize that grace is a gift from God. It is something that we do not deserve but receive. We did not deserve the Holy Spirit to come dwell in us, but we are the recipients of God's grace and mercy. We are the end road of God's mercy. We are to be open to the grace, love, and goodness of the Holy Spirit.

---

3. Karkkainen, *Guide of Christian Theology*, 25.

Conclusion

We have often viewed the Holy Spirit as a tool to help us. But it is not purposed to be a tool. It is a gift, given to us so that we may live more fully and abundantly. The Holy Spirit as grace compels us to action in the world.

The church has somehow forgotten this meaning of the Holy Spirit as a gift to us. We have lost the powerful meaning and place of grace in our lives. Grace embraces us and carries us through the good times and the most difficult times. Grace is abundant for us, and it will free us.

God's grace is transformative. It holds no grudges. It forgives. It heals. It releases one's *han*. It builds bridges. It helps us understand that God is within us. God never leaves us. We need to move forward in understanding that it is the grace within that liberates us and moves us. God's grace comes through the Spirit, which is freely given to us and moves us to work toward justice. God's grace is strong, motivating us to work to make this world a better place. We need to open ourselves to receive God's grace, which will assure us of God's love and mercy for us.

Understanding and embracing the Holy Spirit is important to Christian living today. The Spirit is reflected in our relationships with people, with the planet, and with God. These areas are vitally important, as they are the areas of growth we urgently need to develop. We seek the Spirit to empower us to build a peaceful reign of God's justice on Earth.

The world is torn by injustice, retribution, discrimination, terrorism, and pain. We cause *han* to others. We are at a pivot in the life of humanity, a point where our continued wrong turns may cause irreversible damage to the Earth. We began as a small species in an immense world, but we have proliferated and dominated the Earth like it was ours, creating much *han* to the Earth in just the last 200 years.

Han is presented in the ways that Christians have historically and contemporarily demonized other religions. In the Western world, it is Islam that has been condemned. However, we know that protecting our orthodoxy is not important to a God who says, "I WILL BE WHO I WILL BE." Eurocentric Christianity is not as important as it once was, because Christianity is becoming less relevant to white people in Europe and North America. Yet its relevance is mobilized and moves towards the global South and Bantu, where Afro-Semitic dialects join Spanish, English, German, French, and Dutch dialects as important Christian languages. As Christianity moves southward, we need to recognize the power of spiritualities that have existed in these cultures for thousands of years. As we recognize the breadth and scope of the Holy Spirit experienced by people around the world, we recognize the opportunity to open the Spirit of our own Christian faith.

What Did YOU Do All Day?

Our lives are complicated. We have expectations from many people who also have many expectations of us. There are religious, cultural, familial, and career expectations laid upon us, which work curiously with our own expectations of ourselves.

These social and internal expectations are tested for many people that are leaving nine-to-five careers for freelance work, where they can have more freedom in choosing their schedules. These individuals, such as freelance writers and editors, can give others the impression that they don't have a job.

A few summers ago, my eldest son was enrolled in the Johns Hopkins Summer program for gifted and talented youth. I dropped him off at eight every morning and picked him up at nine every night for three weeks. One morning before I dropped him off, he suddenly asked me to get him a pair of white socks. I told him that I would if I had time to get them.

That day, I was too busy to go to the department store to pick up a pair, so when I picked him up at nine he asked me if I got them.

I said, "Sorry, no."

To my surprise, he then asked me, "What did you even do all day?"

In his mind, he innocently believed that his mother's daily life could not possibly occupy the time it took to adhere to his request. It was a quick response to an idea that as a mother, he had subtle control of his own life through mine.

Humans seek control in every way. In particular, we seek to control the people in our relationships. Sometimes this pursuit is successful. A son pushed by a hopeful parent to become a lawyer may likely become one, or a partner encouraged by a spouse to quit their job after having children may indeed quit a job. However, our desire to control God and the Spirit cannot be satisfied. The Spirit moves as it will, and we have no control. We cannot control the Spirit, but there are ways in which we can be aware of the guidance of the Spirit.

Realizing we have no control of the Spirit is alarming to many people. No control means being at the mercy and grace of God. But we need to be

CONCLUSION

especially open to the movement of the Spirit. The Spirit plays the music of the spheres on its reed pipe, and we need to listen to it and obey its tunes.

Power With

The Spirit is so powerful that it can invert the way we see things. Power is understood in many forms. Starhawk is a theorist of feminist Neopaganism who believes that *power* is another word for energy, the subtle current of forces that shape reality. She differentiates between "power over," "power within," and "power with." "Power over" is the mode of patriarchal societies. It expresses the logic of domination by which some—mostly males—dominate women, subjugate classes, disenfranchise races, and rape the nonhuman world. "Power over" operated in the colonized world, and it has long sustained subordination as colonized societies were rendered powerless. Remnants of that power linger strongly today.

"Power within" is a process by which dominated people relieve themselves of the control of others and their own internalization of the powerlessness projected onto them, laying hold of their innate power and goodness. "Power with" encourages the sharing of power, to affirm oneself while also mutually affirming one another. Here, each person flourishes by promoting the flourishing of others.[4] This type of power is life-giving, sustaining, and encouraging.

The power of the Spirit is "power with." It is a sharing of power as the Spirit vibrates and moves in us so that we become collaborators with the power of the Spirit. It leads to greater accomplishments of us, society, and the world. The Spirit brings forth life-changing power that becomes a transformative and energetic force in our lives. With the transformative power of the Spirit, we can achieve great things.

As Christians, we cannot just think about the Spirit. We need to be able to live with the Spirit, through the Spirit, and by the Spirit for our inner transformation to take place. Only then will the changes we seek in the world take place.

We must allow the Spirit to motivate us and stir us to seek global justice. We must be guided by the Spirit in all that we do. We work with the movement of the Spirit as wind, light, and breath to change us and empower us to be agents of change.

4. Starhawk, *Spiral Dance*, 51.

Reimagining Spirit

When the Spirit fills our lives, we follow the rhythm of the Spirit. We are guided by the Spirit to become new creatures and become agents of change. We become workers in the Spirit and for the Spirit.

Powerful Scriptural Spirit

In the Hebrew Bible, the Spirit empowers the Servant of God to work for justice and peace and to create a community of liberated life (Isa 11). In the New Testament, at Pentecost, there is a powerful outpouring of the Spirit (Acts 2:1–3). The communities of followers of Jesus received the Spirit, which was understood to be the source of an extraordinary power. It is power beyond our worldly comprehension and beyond our worldly expectations. The Spirit empowered and directed the early church.[5] The Spirit that created life, transformed the people, and moved the early church is not gone. Enter now that life of the Spirit.

Christ is portrayed as "a life-giving Spirit" (1 Cor 15:45). The believer has a responsibility to live her life in the power of the Spirit (Rom 8:4–6, 14).[6] This responsibility should not be taken lightly, as one should not ignore the depth of the Spirit's power. Walking in the power of the Spirit is life-changing, as the Spirit becomes an agent through which transformations can occur.

John's letters speak of anointing with the Spirit (1 John 2:20, 27). The Spirit is named the "other Paraclete" (John 14:16), which implies that Jesus is the first (1 John 2:1). The term *parakletos* (from *para+kalein*) means "one called alongside to help," and thus is an advocate or witness (John 14:26).[7] The Spirit may be that Paraclete which becomes a source of inspiration and light as we feel its presence around us. The Spirit becomes a facet of faithful living as an advocate for a life of good stewardship.

The Spirit as light, *chi*, and peace gives us the energy and the power to do the work of God. We are to become the light of the world. The light does not hide under a bushel but shines brightly in the darkness. We are to shine brightly in this broken world to help repair the damage. We are to shout from the mountaintops and declare the goodness of God.

The *chi* is power and life-giving energy. *Chi* in our bodies will give us renewed life and energy to become agents of change. *Chi* requires us to

---

5. Karkkainen, *Guide of Christian Theology*, 6.
6. Karkkainen, *Guide of Christian Theology*, 7.
7. Karkkainen, *Guide of Christian Theology*, 7.

move from the worship halls of raised hands that praise God to the broken world that needs repair. *Chi* will give us the peace to do the healing and repairing that is desperately needed in our world.

Power of the Spirit to Rebuild the Earth

God is the defender of the poor and the oppressed (Jer 9:23). God did not withhold his wrath against those who harmed widows and orphans. Scripture suggests we do the same. It is a commandment from God that all are required to follow and obey. We are to live it out in our lives, and God's Spirit makes it possible.

Under the Spirit's guidance, we can imagine a society that will seek sustainability and equity. We can imagine a society where the community makes decisions to maintain the common good for their people and the Earth. We can recognize that all forms of capital must be considered in the notion of the good life and first is "nature's capital." The good life is dependent on nature's capital. We must resist the tendency to see nature as an inexhaustible commodity. We need to work towards justice as sustainability. We need goals for planetary living that fulfill what Jesus meant by the reign of God.

In many Asian cultures, as with the Israelites of the Old Testament, time is understood as cyclical. Time is happening simultaneously at more than one level. So the past can be present and the present intertwines with the past. There seems to be neither a beginning nor an end. In the West, time is considered to be linear. This makes it difficult to grasp biblical eschatology, where the present and the future—"the now and the not yet"—are seen as interconnected. The study of pneumatology, Spirit and its values, helps us understand how the Advent experience of waiting for God to come and the historical experience of remembering God who has come eventually integrate. It creates an open attitude towards life as a gift, renewing itself from the past and into the future. The Spirit is a movement: the Spirit, who goes between spaces, moves through the interstices of space and time.[8] The Spirit challenges us to recognize that our past and future are connected by God and that both are important for us today.

As we engage in conversations about the Spirit, we recognize that the Holy Spirit transforms us to become the best that we can be by our love. Love is what challenges and moves us toward justice and wholeness. The

---

8. McFague, *Life Abundant*, 122.

power of the Spirit centers us and carries us into the web of life. We are part of creation and creation is part of us.

Love happens in different ways. *Agape* love will move us to move the world. Love changes our world. We need to allow the Spirit to enter our hearts with love and empower us to work for justice. We need to surrender to the Spirit so that we can be filled with the Spirit. The love of the Spirit will empower us to work for God: to generate justice, be merciful, and fill the world with God's love. The Spirit, the power of Eros, makes that possible. This erotic power motivates us and works through us. As we experience God's presence, we each contribute to the building of the reign of God here on Earth. It is a task that calls all of us.

We cannot change our ways alone; we require the power of the Holy Spirit to transform us and help us to move forward to build a sustainable reign of God in this world. We need to work together to save our planet and ourselves. Welcome the Spirit to center us in a vision to find the means we need to build the kin-dom of God.

Understanding and embracing the Holy Spirit is vital to Christian living today. The Spirit is reflected in our relationships with others, with the planet, and with God. These three areas are crucial. It is imperative that we work with the Holy Spirit to change ourselves and our relations.

Surrendering to the Spirit

We desire to control everything. All the variables that we can control in our lives are usually handled with some kind of governance. The time we wake up in the morning; the route we take to work; the food we eat for dinner; or our schedules for the upcoming weeks. We are a society that is buttressed on these little choices, but when we lose a grip on the reins of control, we may go a little crazy. As a mother of three children, I would like to think that I have some kind of control over them. I urge my children to work hard to get good grades at school, meet the right type of friends, and behave in a particular way that I believe is correct. I want them to achieve their own milestones while becoming the best versions of themselves. However, this hoped-for outcome is not limited to their own will, as I am constantly there providing them some kind of influence and some sort of authority.

We cannot behave in such a way with the Spirit. We need to be able to surrender to the Spirit, allowing it to be within us so that we can practice stewardship in this world. We can do this through sustainable living and working towards loving those who are different from us. If the Spirit resides in us, we will recognize the importance of extending grace to the planet. We will recognize that our selfish ways are harmful to the Earth.

My Mother's Last Fight

While we try to maintain control in our lives, we cannot but help to encounter the bountiful surprises that life throws at us. Of course, some of them are good, while others are not so good at all. We will find ourselves reaching moments where we are incredibly joyful, only to get thrown a bombshell that shatters our resolute contentment. Some of these we can control but others we cannot.

When my mother was diagnosed with stage-four lung cancer, my entire world collapsed. At first, the feeling I felt could only be described as numbness. I felt it in my heart wilt, but then that limp numbness soon became replaced with a revival of anger. My mother had done everything right. She always lived a healthy and conscious lifestyle. She never smoked, she exercised regularly, she rarely ate meat, and she even ate all the cancer-preventing foods. So how could she be diagnosed with stage 4 lung cancer at the age of sixty-three?

As my mother went through cancer treatments from both Western and Eastern medicine, our family slowly witnessed her body deteriorate. No treatment was sufficient, as the cancer quickly spread throughout her body. Eventually, it made its way into her brain, and she suffered a stroke that left her immobile and mute. She became like an infant, needing someone to bathe, feed, and change her. She lost all control of her life.

Doctors and psychologists tested her brain capacity and concluded that it was failing. A psychologist did a simple "matching game" exercise with pictures and words to test my mom's cognitive ability. She was unable to do it. She could not comprehend words and was losing control of both her body and mind.

In the last month of her life, our minister came to visit her. As soon as he walked into my mom's room, tears started to roll down her face. The minister asked my sister and I to leave the room. While we waited outside, we pressed in, curious as to what was happening inside the hospital room.

After about twenty-five minutes, our pastor emerged and told us that they had prayed together. With tears in his eyes, he told us that my mother understood the prayer and was at peace. I was cynical, as she could not even understand me anymore. Our pastor left us.

When we re-entered the room, we saw my mom's face. Her eyes were bloodshot and glassy, her nose was red, and she had tissues scattered all over her lap and around her blankets. However, I noticed that her demeanor had changed, and for the first time since her diagnosis, I saw a sense of genuine peace on her face. For the past six months, she had been tirelessly fighting her cancer and desperately wanted to beat it. Watching her experience, it was clear to me that she was afraid to die. She had no peace.

But in her conversation and prayer with the pastor, in the midst of her terminal illness, she had been able to come to accept her death, finally finding peace with herself. She surrendered to God and was able to come to terms with the reality that she would not live much longer. She realized that the Spirit of God was within her, and found inner calm within this acceptance. Two weeks later, she passed away.

I know how difficult it is to surrender fully to the Spirit. It requires a lot from us, especially when we want so much to control, predict, and have power over our lives. But unless we surrender to the Spirit, the Spirit is not free to move in our lives. Without surrendering our desire for control and allowing the Spirit to control our lives, we are unable to move our hearts for change.

My mother surrendered to the Spirit, and the Spirit gave her a peace that no one else could offer. This grace enabled her to let go of earthly things. This peaceful grace enabled her to surrender to God.

The Spirit provides peace, grace, and mercy in our lives. As the Spirit moves, it can help us transform each other and the world. We need to allow the Spirit to enter our lives to help us release our *han*. Without surrendering ourselves, it is difficult to allow the Spirit to move within our lives. Without the Spirit releasing this *han*, we will not find peace, serenity, or grace in our lives.

The Holy Spirit is not like the Spirit that was part of my childhood, a Spirit that terrified me and made me assume that Christians were all crazy people. But now, we are talking about a Spirit that is vibration, light, breath, and wind, which transforms our inner selves so that we can do what is right and work for justice to make this world a kin-dom of God.

CONCLUSION

Powerful Scriptural Spirit

Christ is portrayed as "a life-giving Spirit" (1 Cor 15:45). The believer has a responsibility to live her life in the power of the Spirit (Rom 8:4–6, 14).[9] This responsibility should not be taken lightly, as one should not ignore the depth of the Spirit's power. Walking in the power of the Spirit is life-changing, as the Spirit becomes an agent through which transformations can occur.

The Spirit as light and *chi*, a spirit of peace, gives us the energy and the power to do the work of God. We are to become the light of the world. The light does not hide under a bushel but rather shines brightly in the darkness. We are to shine brightly in this broken world to help repair the damage.

The *chi* is power and life-giving energy. *Chi* in our bodies will give us renewed life and energy to become agents of change. *Chi* requires us to move from the worship halls of raised hands that praise God to the realities of our broken world in desperate need of repair. *Chi* will give us the peace to do the healing and the repairing that is gravely needed in our world.

Power of the Spirit to Rebuild the Earth

God is the defender of the poor and the oppressed (Jer 9:23). God did not withhold his wrath from those who harmed widows and orphans. Defending the poor and the oppressed is a commandment from God that all are required to follow and obey. We are to live it out in our lives, and God's Spirit makes it possible.

With the Spirit's leading, we can imagine a society that will seek sustainability and equity. We can imagine a society where the community makes decisions on how to maintain the common good and the Earth. We can recognize that all forms of capital must be considered in the notion of the good life, and the first is "nature's capital." The good life is dependent upon nature's capital. We must resist the tendency to see nature as an inexhaustible commodity. We need to work towards justice as sustainability, the goals for planetary living to fulfill what Jesus meant by the reign of God.

The study of pneumatology, of the Spirit and its values, helps us understand how the Advent experience of waiting for God to come and the historical experience of remembering the God who has come amalgamate

---

9. Karkkainen, *Guide of Christian Theology*, 7.

to create an open attitude towards life as a gift, renewing itself from the past and into the future. The Spirit is a movement: the Spirit, who goes between spaces, moves through the borders of space and time.[10] The Spirit challenges us to recognize that our past and future are one and that both are important for us today.

As we engage in conversation about the Spirit, we recognize that this Spirit transforms us to become the best that we can be by our love. Love is the force that challenges us to move towards justice and wholeness. The power of the Spirit centers us and brings us into the interconnectedness of all life on Earth. We are part of creation, and creation is part of us.

Within creation is love. Love happens in different ways. *Agape* love will move us to move the world. Love changes our world. The love from the Spirit will empower us to work for God to be just, merciful, and to fill the world with God's love. The Spirit, the power of Eros, makes that possible. This erotic power motivates us and works through us. As we experience God's presence, we each contribute to the building of the reign of God here on Earth. It is a task that requires all of us in order to succeed.

---

10. McFague, *Life Abundant*, 122.

Bibliography

Badman, Keith. *The Beach Boys: The Definitive Diary of America's Greatest Band on Stage and in the Studio*. Perth: Backbeat, 2004.

Botelho, Greg. "What Happened the Night Trayvon Martin Died." *CNN*, May 23, 2012. Online. https://www.cnn.com/2012/05/18/justice/florida-teen-shooting-details/index.html.

Brainard, Lael, et al. *Climate Change and Global Poverty: A Billion Lives in the Balance?* Washington, DC: Brookings Institution, 2009.

Britain Yearly Meeting. "Reflections." In *Quaker Faith and Practice: The Book of Christian Discipline of the Yearly Meeting of the Religious Society of Friends (Quakers) in Britain*, §26. Online. https://qfp.quaker.org.uk/chapter/26.

Calvin, John. *Institutes of the Christian Religion*. Translated by Henry Beveridge. Grand Rapids: Eerdmans, 1972.

Cerullo, Megan. "Unarmed Black Man Shot to Death in His Own Backyard after Police Mistake Cell Phone for Weapon." *Daily News*, March 20, 2018. Online. http://www.nydailynews.com/news/national/unarmed-black-man-shot-death-backyard-article-1.3886562.

Chase, Randal S. *New Testament Study Guide, Pt. 2: The Infinite Atonement/Acts of the Apostles*. Washington, UT: Plain and Precious, 2011.

Chung, Christopher K., and Samson Cho. "The Significance of *Jeong* in Korean Culture and Psychotherapy." Harbor-UCLA Medical Center. Online. www.prcp.org/publications/sig.pdf.

Chung, Hyun Kyung. "Ecology, Feminism, and African and Asian Spirituality: Towards a Spirituality of Eco-Feminism." In *Ecotheology: Voices from South and North*, edited by David G. Hallman, 175–78. Maryknoll, NY: Orbis, 1994.

Cobb, John B., Jr. "The Holy Spirit and the Present Age." In *The Lord and Giver of Life: Perspectives on Constructive Pneumatology*, edited by David H. Jensen, 147–62. Louisville: Westminster John Knox, 2008.

Cohen, Kenneth S. *The Way of Qigong: The Art and Science of Chinese Energy Healing*. Toronto: Wellspring/Ballantine, 2018.

Columbia University Press. "Shekinah." In *The Columbia Encyclopedia*. 6th ed. New York: Columbia University Press, 2019. Online. https://www.encyclopedia.com/philosophy-and-religion/judaism/judaism/shekinah.

Bibliography

Derr, Eric. "California Lawmakers Pass Statewide Ban on One-Use Plastic Bags." *Latin Post*, September 1, 2014. Online. https://www.latinpost.com/articles/20509/20140901/california-lawmakers-pass-statewide-ban-on-one-use-plastic-bags.htm.

Eck, Diana L. *Encountering God: A Spiritual Journey from Bozeman to Banaras*. Boston: Beacon, 2003.

Enos, Olivia. "Nearly Two-Thirds of Human Trafficking Victims Are from Asia." *The Daily Signal*, November 20, 2014. Online. https://www.dailysignal.com/2014/11/20/nearly-two-thirds-human-trafficking-victims-asia.

"Family of Unarmed Black Man Shot at Walmart Demands Police Release Dashcam Video." *ABC News*, April 20, 2018. Online. https://abcnews.go.com/US/family-unarmed-black-man-shot-walmart-demands-police/story?id=54603667.

Fowler, Tara, and Nicole Weisensee Egan. "CNN's Don Lemon Apologizes After Telling Bill Cosby Accuser How to Avoid Rape." *People*, November 19, 2014. Online. https://people.com/tv/cnns-don-lemon-apologizes-after-telling-bill-cosby-accuser-how-to-avoid-rape.

Gillet, Richard W. *The New Globalization: Reclaiming the Lost Ground of Our Christian Social Tradition*. Cleveland: Pilgrim, 2005.

Goldberg, David Theo. "Heterogeneity and Hybridity: Colonial Legacy, Postcolonial Heresy." In *A Companion to Postcolonial Studies*, edited by Henry Schwarz and Sangeeta Ray, 72–86. Malden, MA: Blackwell, 2000.

Guthrie, Kenneth Sylvan, ed. *The Pythagorean Sourcebook and Library*. Edited and introduced by David Fideler. Kindle ed. Grand Rapids: Phanes, 1988.

Hodgson, Peter C. *Christian Faith: A Brief Introduction*. Louisville: Westminster John Knox, 2001.

Jenkins, Philip. *The New Faces of Christianity*. Oxford: Oxford University Press, 2008.

Jensen, David H. "Discerning the Spirit: A Historical Introduction." In *The Lord and Giver of Life: Perspectives on Constructive Pneumatology*, edited by David H. Jensen, 1–24. Louisville: Westminster John Knox, 2008.

Karkkainen, Veli-Matti. *A Guide to Christian Theology: The Holy Spirit*. Louisville: Westminster John Knox, 2012.

———. *Pneumatology: The Holy Spirit in Ecumenical, International, and Contextual Perspective*. Grand Rapids: Baker Academic, 2018.

Kerber, Guillermo. "Time to Convert to Climate Justice." *Church Times*, March 21, 2014. Online. https://www.churchtimes.co.uk/articles/2014/21-march/comment/opinion/time-to-convert-to-climate-justice.

Kim, Grace Ji-Sun. "Care for the Whole Creation: The World Council of Churches at COP20 in Lima. *Huffington Post*, December 17, 2014. Online. https://www.huffpost.com/entry/care-for-the-whole-creation_6334298.

———. *Colonialism, Han, and the Transformative Spirit*. New York: Palgrave Macmillan, 2013.

———. *The Grace of Sophia*. Cleveland: Pilgrim, 2002.

———. *The Holy Spirit, Chi, and the Other: A Model of Global and Intercultural Pneumatology*. New York: Palgrave, 2011.

———. "Uncovering Bill Cosby's Feet of Clay with Allegations of Sexual Assaults." *Feminist Studies in Religion*, December 3, 2014. Online. https://www.fsrinc.org/uncovering-bill-cosbys-feet-clay-allegations-sexual-assault.

———. "Walls That Divide." *Sojourners* (blog), March 11, 2014. Online. https://sojo.net/articles/walls-divide.

Bibliography

———. "What Forms Us: Multiculturalism, the Other, and Theology." In *Feminist Theology With A Canadian Accent: Canadian Perspectives on Contextual Theology*, edited by Mary Ann Beavis, Elaine Guillemin, and Barbara Pell, 78–99. Ottawa: Novalis, 2008.

Kim, Grace Ji-Sun, and Hilda P. Koster. *Planetary Solidarity: Global Women's Voices on Christian Doctrine and Climate Justice*. Minneapolis: Fortress, 2017.

Klostermaier, Klaus K. *A Survey of Hinduism*. Albany, NY: State University of New York Press, 2007.

Knightley, Philip. "Longtime Australian Policy: Kidnapping Children from Families." *Center for Public Integrity*, February 8, 2001. Online. https://publicintegrity.org/accountability/longtime-australian-policy-kidnapping-children-from-families.

Kwok, Pui-Lan. *Postcolonial Imagination and Feminist Theology*. Louisville: Westminster John Knox, 2005.

Martin, Philip. "Scalping: Fact and Fantasy." In *Rethinking Columbus: The Next 500 Years*, edited by Bill Bieglow and Bob Peterson, 58–59. 2nd ed. Milwaukee: Rethinking Schools, 1998.

McFague, Sallie. "The Dearest Freshness Deep Down Things: Some Reflections on the Holy Spirit and Climate Change." In *The Lord and Giver of Life: Perspectives on Constructive Pneumatology*, edited by David H. Jensen, 113–28. Louisville: Westminster John Knox, 2008.

———. *Life Abundant: Rethinking Theology and Economy for a Planet in Peril*. Minneapolis: Fortress, 2001.

———. *A New Climate for Theology: God, the World, and Global Warming*. Minneapolis: Fortress, 2008.

Mendelsohn, Robert. "Development in the Balance: Agriculture and Water." In *Climate Change and Global Poverty: A Billion Lives in the Balance?*, edited by Lael Brainard, Abigail Jones, and Nigel Purvis, 120–29. Washington, DC: Brookings Institution, 2009.

Miller, George. *The Skekinah Glory*. Maitland, FL: Xulon, 2007.

Min, Anselm. *The Solidarity of Others in a Divided World: A Postmodern Theology After Postmodernism*. New York: T & T Clark, 2001.

Moe-Lobeda, Cynthia D. *Healing a Broken World: Globalization and God*. Minneapolis: Fortress, 2002.

Moltmann, Jürgen. *The Source of Life: The Holy Spirit and the Theology of Life*. Minneapolis: Fortress, 1997.

———. *The Spirit of Life: A Universal Affirmation*. Translated by Margaret Kohl. Minneapolis: Fortress, 1992.

O'Murchu, Diarmuid. *In the Beginning Was the Spirit: Science, Religion, and Indigenous Spirituality*. Maryknoll, NY: Orbis, 2012.

Pannenberg, Wolfhart. *Systematic Theology*. Grand Rapids: Eerdmans, 1994.

Parenti, Christian. *Tropic of Chaos: Climate Change and the New Geography of Violence*. New York: Nation, 2011.

Park, Andrew Sung. *From Hurt to Healing: A Theology of the Wounded*. Nashville: Abingdon, 2004.

———. *The Wounded Heart of God: The Asian Concept of Han and the Christian Doctrine of Sin*. Nashville: Abingdon, 1993.

Peglar, Tori. "1995 Reintroduction of Wolves in Yellowstone." *My Yellowstone*, July 23, 2018. Online. https://www.yellowstonepark.com/park/yellowstone-wolves-reintroduction.

Bibliography

Placher, William C. *The Triune God: An Essay in Postliberal Theology*. Louisville: Westminster John Knox, 2007.

Pullella, Philip. "Pope Francis 'Prayer' Request to Journalists: 'Send Me Good Vibrations.'" *Huffington Post*, June 8, 2015. Online. http://www.huffingtonpost.com/2015/06/08/pope-francis-good-vibrations_n_7535770.html?ncid=fcbklnkushpmg00000051.

Pungur, Joseph. *Theology Interpreted*. Lanham, MD: University Press of America, 1993.

Ruether, Rosemary Radford. *Integrating Ecofeminism, Globalization, and World Religions*. Lanham, MD: Rowman and Littlefield, 2005.

Smith, Andrea. *Conquest: Sexual Violence and American Indian Genocide*. Durham, NC: Duke University Press, 2015.

Starhawk. *The Spiral Dance: A Rebirth of the Ancient Religion of the Great Goddess*. New York: Harper-Collins, 1989.

Stevenson, Leslie. *Open to New Light: Quaker Spirituality in Historical and Philosophical Context*. Luton: Andrews UK, 2011.

Sugirtharajah, R. S. *The Bible and The Third World: Precolonial, Colonial, and Postcolonial Encounters*. Cambridge: Cambridge University Press, 2001.

Thurman, Howard. *Jesus and the Disinherited*. Boston: Beacon, 1996.

Torrance, T. F. *The Trinitarian Faith*. Edinburgh: T & T Clark, 1988.

United Nations Population Fund (UNFPA). *State of the World Population: Women, Population, and Climate Change*. New York: UNFPA, 2009.

Wallace, Mark I. "Spirit." In *Constructive Theology: A Contemporary Approach to Classical Themes*, edited by Serene Jones and Paul Lakeland, 238–79. Minneapolis: Augsburg Fortress, 2005.

Wang, Frances Kai-Hwa. "Who Is Vincent Chin? The History and Relevance of a 1982 Killing." *NBC News*, June 15, 2017. Online. http://www.nbcnews.com/news/asian-america/who-vincent-chin-history-relevance-1982-killing-n771291.

Weber, Max. *The Protestant Ethic and the Spirit of Capitalism*. London: Routledge, 1992.

White House, Office of the Press Secretary. "President Bush Signs Secure Fence Act." *White House*, October 26, 2006. Online. https://georgewbush-whitehouse.archives.gov/news/releases/2006/10/20061026.html.

Whitehead, Alfred North. *Process and Reality*. Kindle ed. New York: Simon and Schuster, 2010.

Wong, Eva. *Being Taoist: Wisdom for Living a Balanced Life*. Kindle ed. Boston: Shambhala, 2015.

Woodley, Randy S. "Native American Christianity: Through Bullets and Arrows to Peace." *Huffington Post*, October 27, 2012. Online. https://www.huffingtonpost.com/rev-dr-randy-s-woodley/native-american-christianity-through-bullets-and-arrows-to-peace_b_1826126.html.

World Council of Churches (WCC). "What Is the World Council of Churches?" *Oikoumene*. Online. https://www.oikoumene.org/en/about-us.

World Health Organization (WHO). *Gender, Climate Change, and Health*. Geneva: World Health Organization, 2011.

Wright, N. T. *New Heavens, New Earth: The Biblical Picture of Christian Hope*. Cambridge: Grove, 1999.

Young, Robert. *Colonial Desire: Hybridity in Theory, Culture, and Race*. London: Routledge, 2008.

Yun, Koo D. "Pneumatological Perspectives on World Religions: The Cosmic Spirit and Ch'i." In *Asian Contextual Theology for the Third Millennium: Theology of Minjung*

in *Fourth-Eye Formation*, edited by Paul S. Chung, Kim Kyoung-Jae, and Veli-Matti Karkkainen, 165–78. Eugene, OR: Pickwick, 2007.
Zukowski, Dan. "5.0 Earthquake Hits Oklahoma, Continuing String of Fracking-Induced Shakes." *Nation of Change*, November 7, 2016. Online. https://www.nationofchange.org/2016/11/07/5-0-earthquake-hits-oklahoma-continuing-trend-fracking-induced-shakes.

www.ingramcontent.com/pod-product-compliance
Lightning Source LLC
Chambersburg PA
CBHW022130160426
43197CB00009B/1217